Other books by Manès Sperber:

Abyss
The Achilles Heel
Burned Bramble
Journey Without End
Lost Bay
Man and His Deeds

MASKS OF LONELINESS

MASKS OF LONELINESS

ALFRED ADLER IN PERSPECTIVE

MANÈS SPERBER

Translation by Krishna Winston

Macmillan Publishing Co., Inc.

NEW YORK

Translation copyright © 1974 by Macmillan Publishing Co., Inc.

Macmillan Publishing Co., Inc.
866 Third Avenue, New York, N. Y. 10022

Library of Congress Cataloging in Publication Data

Sperber, Manès, 1905-
  Masks of loneliness.

  1. Adler, Alfred, 1870-1937. I. Title.
BF109.A4S63   150'.19'53   73-13167
ISBN 0-02-612950-7

First Printing

Printed in the United States of America

Masks of Loneliness was originally published under the German title, *Alfred Adler oder das Elend der Psychologie.* Copyright © 1970 by Manès Sperber.

Excerpt on page 71 reprinted by permission of the estate of Alfred Adler. From *Understanding Human Nature* by Alfred Adler, copyright © 1927, 1954 by Kurt A. Adler.

Excerpt on pages 132-133 from Alfred Adler, *The Practice and Theory of Individual Psychology.* New York: Humanities Press, Inc.

There is no absolute truth,
but what comes closest to it
is the human community.

—ALFRED ADLER

Contents

Part Four

Foreword

As a ten-year-old I took careful note of the date, and today, over fifty years later, I have not forgotten it: on July 27, 1916 we finally arrived in Vienna—after an adventurous, needlessly roundabout escape. My parents feared the unknown and the deprivations it would bring, and perhaps they suspected that once they reached the big city even the desire to return to their home would desert them. In fact they did not leave Vienna until twenty-three years later, one day after the outbreak of World War II. And they never did return, either to their little town or to Austria.

That first summer I spent many hot afternoons in the Prater, wandering among the booths where the *artistes* cried their wares, in an effort to attract the scanty weekday audience. The heat made the red, yellow and white greasepaint on their faces smear into weird and terrifying designs. They never played out the sensational dramas they promised; they strained their voices in vain, for we were not to be transformed into paying customers. Occasionally someone would decide to risk the entrance fee:

a lonely soldier on leave or a down-in-the dumps war veteran.

One evening several violent downpours had emptied out the Prater even before darkness, and I was on my way home when I experienced one of those moments in which a sudden realization presents itself so forcefully that one stops dead in one's tracks. I suddenly grasped why I had wasted week after week in the Prater: I had not wanted to admit to myself how much the city disappointed me.

Jerusalem. Vienna. These two names had represented magical places in my childhood daydreams, places at once very near and very far. I knew that Jerusalem existed in time and could never be lost, for God himself had promised it to us. But Vienna existed in the space to which we belonged, the empire of Franz Joseph, whose subjects we were. It would be a city of palaces, built not of bricks and stone but of gleaming crystals, a city on which night never dared to descend. To the child in a distant province, the Imperial City suggested glory and splendor, absolute terrestrial beauty; but now reality had unmasked and destroyed the dream. Nothing could equal the image a lively imagination had created—not the Old or the New Hofburg with its famed changing of the guard, not the Cathedral of St. Stephen or the imposing Ministry of War, before which crowds sometimes gathered of an evening to hear reports of gallant victories. And the Viennese themselves were not what they should have been: that I recognized, once the illusion had been shattered.

To this day I recall the precise spot on the Praterstrasse, opposite the Carl Theater, where it suddenly became clear that I would have to learn to live on the debris of my illusions, and I wondered then why it should be as difficult to live with an illusion as without one. Since that day I have never ceased searching for the answer. It took me five years, until the autumn of 1921, to understand the possibilities and difficulties involved in finding one; then, before I was even sixteen years old, I met Dr. Alfred Adler at an evening adult education course. At the time he was fifty-one and thus had the major part of his life behind him.

As I recollect, the course took place on Monday evenings in a classroom of the *Sophiengymnasium* in Vienna's Second District. I came there to learn, but also to discuss, to express my doubts, even to attack—for I had already traveled a long road. The five years since my first summer in Vienna had been filled to the brim with events, adventures and experiences. We had all lived through the "last days of mankind," [1] and had survived—but in what a state!

Innumerable details have been recorded by contemporary journalists, memoirists and historians, but anyone who experienced the hunger and the cold in wartorn Vienna knows that an adequate account of those days may never be given. The situation was desperate but certainly not serious—that was the joke that made the rounds of the cafés, where the miserable lighting inspired the patrons to new heights of gallows humor. The Habsburg Empire had romped through its declining years with jubilees and innumerable festivals, sloppily organized but nevertheless successful; now it expired amid such misery, such shabbiness, that we young people were inclined to believe that nothing had ever been real except the Lipizzan horses of the Spanish Riding School; it had all been a façade, a hocus-pocus. Elsewhere [2] I have described how my generation learned to question everything. We were convinced that even the most stubborn problems could be solved by the courage and perspicacity of those who were truly altruistic, who considered poverty not an unpleasant absence of wealth but the liberating condition that would eliminate what Marx had called reification—the dominance of material things over man. We believed that human beings would soon cease to be the slaves of objects. This generation felt that it had a rendezvous with the boldest truths, with answers to questions it thought it had discovered.

Obsessed with the future, which it heralds and from which it awaits confirmation, revolutionary youth always turns toward the past: it seeks its prophets and its heroes in forgotten graves. In this spirit the youth of the defeated countries combed the history books after World War I. They read Marx and his disciples, but at the same time they gobbled up *The Decline of the West*, although they despised the "fine gentlemen" who cited Spengler as an authority. These young people smiled at the sociological ignorance and the political naïveté of Nietzsche, but it was from his philosophy more than from historical materialism that they gained the conviction they would have to break radically with the morality of the past. These young men and women set about analyzing the hierarchical values they had inherited, with an eye to putting them out of circulation for good. Nietzsche's assertion that Socrates was nothing but an exceptionally vocal Sophist was something they took for gospel truth, but they continued to honor the philosopher who had demonstrated how men should die with dignity. They were familiar with Plato's epistemological and political theories and rejected them, but they found poetic visions in the writings of this man who had . claimed to disdain poets. They identified with Spartacus, with Francis of Assisi, with Spinoza, with Saint-Just, with Rosa Luxemburg, with the young terrorists of nineteenth-century Russia, on the one hand; and with Rembrandt, van

Gogh, Cézanne and other unrecognized geniuses, on the other.

My generation thought it was the first to live consciously in a time-space coordinate: all ages were ours, for we felt ourselves to be brotherly contemporaries of all who had preceded us. Whether pupils of Sigmund Freud or of Alfred Adler, we listened to their teachings as if they were only the articulated echo of our own intuition. Everything revealed itself to us as a dialectical unity; all was movement, and only that which was movement existed.

Here I could smoothly fade in: a stocky man standing at a blackboard draws a neat white line from bottom to top. Firmly, as though this line provided incontrovertible evidence, he remarks: "You see, that is the life of the psyche. Everything psychic is movement and must be understood as a movement from below to above." A good number of Adler's audience may have come for the sake of that one word: movement. It was a simple yet universal key.

One heard that Dr. Alfred Adler was a famous man, far more important than his appearance suggested—for he looked like a petty bourgeois Viennese. He also spoke and dressed that way; even his face bore an unmistakable resemblance to the "eternal Viennese," whose sympathetically caricatured features one constantly encountered in newspapers and on posters. At first one did not find him impressive. But if one observed him closely, one noticed that he had remarkable eyes: their expression changed with unusual, sometimes startling rapidity. The gaze of an attentive, kindly man could suddenly become piercing, even hostile, before it underwent another equally sudden transformation and finally turned away entirely.

Adler had a remarkable effect on anyone who had dealings with him, especially on the young people who came to learn from him. Even after a very brief conversation one went away filled with new faith in oneself, with indistinct but firm hopes for one's own near or distant future—and not because one thought one might thenceforth expect more of others. All of a sudden one realized one had to demand more of oneself, summon up more strength and courage than one had ever thought possible. Many felt they had become different, better, more intelligent and active members of the human community. And this feeling could last an evening, a day, a week, sometimes longer. It would fade gradually, but often it lingered on and never completely vanished.

Adler's biographers, especially the women among them, often lyrically praise his "aura." Their descriptions may be naïve or exaggerated, but in essence they are perfectly true. Anyone who approached Adler free of distrust or dislike would be received in a genuinely Socratic manner. This manner enabled Adler to make even the most insignificant person feel he would talk with Adler as with an equal. Adler was certainly a highly ambitious man, with a controlled but by no means quiescent will-to-power, but his manner went beyond a mere technique for quickly establishing contact; it was the outcome of his philosophy of life and an expression of his nature: he actually perceived every person as his equal.

Socrates was undoubtedly intelligent enough not to lose track of his own wisdom in the course of his endless debates; he did not need advice from the Delphic Oracle. But in conversations he always behaved as though the other person knew as much as he and only needed a hint to arrive at conclusions as wise and as sound as those of the wisest of

Greeks. Unlike the professional Sophists, he did not use dialectics to make the other person furnish the cues for his own monologues; he employed dialogue to dramatize the puzzling dialectic of the fact that every person is at once an *I* and a *you*. And that is why Socrates did not write; he needed the physical presence of an opponent, a partner, whereas a writer like Plato spun out his own monologue in the dramatic form of the drama and dialogue.

Since every advantage has its drawbacks, one may assume that Adler's Socratic nature was the chief reason for his failure to capture in writing what he could convey so convincingly and impressively in conversation.

It is about half a century since this Socratic master drew me into conversation. Our dialogue lasted just over a decade. As I set out to write once more about him and his teachings [3] and about my present view of psychology as applied knowledge of human nature, memories of those distant times awaken in me, memories of that little but great man.

Disagreements, bitter dissension, the wordless break he intentionally brought about five years before his premature death—none of these things can diminish the certainty that came to me on a cold autumn evening in 1921: the certainty that Alfred Adler was an extraordinary teacher, master and friend to his disciples, as long as he trusted them and felt buoyed up by their trust. From him we learned once and for all that an opinion is nothing by comparison with knowledge, and that all knowledge without understanding remains fragmentary. He taught each of us to recognize his own inadequacy and at the same time to make peace with it so that we could overcome it, compensate for it, sometimes overcompensate. In the same breath he taught us to see both the incredible insignificance and the incomparable grandeur of man.

In his best moments Adler showed by his own example that a person who has seen through man's dodges and strategems can still love man—not in spite of this insight but because of it.

I am writing this book under the continued influence of those best moments, and in memory of them.

Part One

Introduction

WHETHER MAN is a wolf to man,[1] a "laughingstock or a searing shame," [2] a challenge, a comfort, or a source of gnawing doubt—one thing is certain: man is a riddle hiding behind a false solution. We think we know the answer before we even know what the riddle is.

Psychology is both the science of man as a riddle and the theory of man's discovery of himself in others. Man is simultaneously and inextricably psychology's subject and its object. This is the first grave problem confronting psychology: the greatest obstacle the psychologist encounters is himself. His anxieties and limitations, secrets and fascinations—all these elements can be found concealed, "objectified," diluted, or generalized in what he presents as an objective picture of man.

As I sit down to describe what strikes me as significant and important about interpretive psychology, and especially about individual psychology and its founder, Alfred Adler, my ideas have been filtered by years of events and experiences. What plagues me is suspicion of the psychologist, and of course that includes the psychologist who is writing these lines.

Where should I begin? With psychology or with the psychologist? If I try to find the proper answer, I condemn myself to running around in circles. How could one even describe a psychologist or interpret his character and his work without applying his own doctrine to him? But if a given psychological system is largely determined—and partially distorted—by the character of the psychologist, who in turn is limited by his subjectivity, how can one trust it as an analytic tool?

Every human being represents a certainty for himself, an eternal presence. Every person experiences himself as a whole, a continent clearly set off from other continents. Any shaking of this certainty is unbearable to us—a grave threat to our identity with ourselves, with the person who by saying "I" announces his uniqueness. For although there are billions of human beings, each of whom says "I," each individual feels himself to be unique, for he is nonreproducible.

This very certainty is an obstacle to the young psychologist, for he must proceed from the assumption that no human being really knows himself fully, without misconceptions, down into the darkest recesses of his soul. The psychologist's very point of departure is already dubious and contradictory: on the basis of experience he posits certainty about oneself and uncertainty about everyone else. But without this contradiction one never catches a glimpse through that narrow door which has the strange property of making every glimpse of the outside simultaneously a glimpse into ourselves. We know that man is a riddle, or can become one, yet at the same time we think we know ourselves and those with whom we come in contact. Something unusual must occur before we are overwhelmed with uncertainty about ourselves and suddenly feel as though we were losing the ground under our feet.

Every science tries to find verifiable answers to legitimate and correctly stated questions. The researcher seeks the causes, purposes and contexts of phenomena that would remain the same even if he did not exist. The true psychologist, on the other hand, starts by asking himself his own questions, by investigating the mind that will do the investigating, by shaking the basic certainty of the person who says "I," by regarding its identity as dubious because not yet proven.

Does one become a psychologist because one is no longer sure of oneself and of those around one on whom one depends and whose actions and reactions one must be able to predict? In order to act rationally, one must know in advance how others will act under certain conditions, but one must also know who and what one is to them, how they regard one, and how to elicit their sympathy or hostility. Thus self-knowledge helps one understand others, and knowledge of human nature helps one understand oneself. If you want a person to listen to you, talk to him about himself!

A person probably wants to become a psychologist in the first place because of a deep interest in himself. But he only becomes a real psychologist if on the way to himself he discovers others and from then on devotes the kind of earnest attention to them that most people devote only to themselves. Usually the first thing that motivates a man to become a psychologist is a sort of psychic earthquake. He has always seen himself as a whole continent; now he finds out that he may be only an archipelago, a whole one, perhaps, but clumsily patched together out of fragments. This earthquake has an enormous impact, the most frightening aspect of which is loss of the ability to take anything for granted.

This loss is connected with the would-be psychologist's second motive, caused by entirely different factors. His relations to others—to his mother, father, sisters and brothers —suddenly become dubious; he had thought of himself as an inseparable part of his environment, and suddenly he sees it as an enemy. His first experience of presumed betrayal makes him lose his sense of being sheltered. He thinks he has been thrown out of the nest. He no longer belongs to anyone, only to himself. But this self has also ceased to provide any certainty.

From this vantage point one can grasp how the individual's two fundamental systems of reference interlock. One system regulates the relationship of the individual to himself, while the other regulates his relationship to those around him. The moment he becomes the *other*—even just in an experiment—other human beings do not come any closer, they do not take the place of his self; rather, his selfhood gets lost. When he loses track of himself, he also loses track of the world. And similarly, he feels lost when he thinks he has been robbed of the love of his parents or when he begins to fear he is not his parents' child and does not belong to his brothers and sisters, that he belongs nowhere.

These interlocking systems of reference are the precondition for any sense of security, of basking in an integrated identity. But this identity is always threatened. From one moment to the next a child can lose it and be overwhelmed with one of the most oppressive anxieties there is: the sense of being exposed, defenseless, utterly alone, rejected and betrayed by the whole world.

Anyone who believes he has suffered this sort of irrevo- cable loss will thenceforth regard the world through dif- ferent eyes. Even when everything seems to return to normal, as often happens with children, even when trust is restored, the process once initiated cannot be halted. One could call it the process of dissolution. It has been known since psychology began in the time of Socrates, and it has often been condemned. All real psychologists, but espe- cially those of our century, have been accused of dissolving basic certainties and of having no other goal than to de- stroy existing values, society, the state, the purity of the soul, of children, of love, and so on.

In the realm of consciousness and introspection not a single step forward can be taken without something's being dissolved—that is, without analysis. The "riddle of man" cannot be deciphered or guessed without man's being changed in the process. We are told that the Sphinx lay in wait for the wanderer outside the gates of Thebes and presented him with riddles, usually childish and ridicu- lously easy ones. But if someone guessed the answer, she hurled herself into the abyss, for without a secret she was nothing.

What does psychology dissolve, the psychology that looks for knowledge of human nature? Its opponents used to think of it as the enemy of religion, of tradition, of re- spect for institutions, the hierarchy of the generations and the sacredness of authority in the family, the school, so- ciety and especially the state—an indictment much more justified than the opponents of psychology realized. In- terpretive psychology was and is guilty of trying to dis- solve all these things. That becomes clear when one re- alizes how it functions.

It dissolves the established form of human existence

within stable relationships and institutions, replacing it with a state of flux. Any moment in which the individual is observed and labelled represents merely one point on the line of his circuitous, often aberrant, and only seemingly consistent movement. It is obvious, for instance, that no institution can afford to be portrayed in the process of formation; every authority claims to have sprung full-blown from the head of Zeus, as it were. And one can hardly worship a monarch if one sees him before one's mind's eye as a naked and squalling infant.

Psychology constantly reminds the individual of his childhood, that being the only way it can strip existence of its false certainties, of the illusion of stability.

Psychology further proceeds from the assumption that what presents itself as reality was not absolutely necessary and need not be real, in the simple sense of the word. The psychologist sees psychic existence as full of illusion, and hopes to dissect this hybrid combination of illusion and reality into its component parts. By uncovering the part played by illusion in our character, our actions and the image we convey through words and gesture, psychology shatters our façades.

Modern psychology has banished from nurseries and bedrooms the theatrical lighting that obscured more than it illuminated. It used to be considered an indisputable truth that childhood was the happiest time of life, and, the relationship between children and their parents was held to be one of filial and parental love. In falsified retrospect, everyday life faded away and with it all its real conflicts—and yet for thousands of years literature has been portraying the force and impact of conflict in fairy tales and epics, in dramas and novels. The ability of almost everyone to ignore obtrusive realities and embrace illusions as if they represented real existence creates a Hydra-headed obstacle that seems to have renewed itself with each new generation.

Our most remarkable and most horrifying trait is our capacity for misinterpreting our own acts, both before and after we have committed them. There is a German proverb: "When two do the same thing it is not the same thing." This suggests that although deeds are usually thought to be unambiguous, they require interpretation before their meaning can be established, and that is often difficult. One could formulate a parallel to that old saying: when two do something different, it may be the same at bottom. Just as one can mislead people with the truth, one can conceal one's character by means of deeds, drowning reality in appearance.

It used to be accepted that the important thing was to distinguish clearly between good and evil, and that a person was either all one or the other. In the folk psychology that has been practiced since human interaction began, the absolute adjectives receive great stress: good and evil, modest and vain, friendly and hostile, peaceable and belligerent, industrious and lazy—those are a few. Of course they are still used today, but they are losing more and more of their expressiveness. If one compares a nineteenth-century novel like *David Copperfield* to a novel of our own day, one sees at once that the modern writer has neither the inclination nor the ability to portray totally good or evil characters. The heroes of novels still perform deeds which one could describe with absolute adjectives, but we know that these adjectives tell us little about the heroes themselves. Man is not his deed—this insight which most modern readers take for granted would have been barely comprehensible and certainly not acceptable to readers of two hundred years ago.

Close investigation of the complicated relationship between man and his deeds destroys a model on which have been based practically all concepts of morality and justice, of crime and punishment. In the particular light of our present knowledge of human nature, crimes still exist; in fact they have become more prominent, but the criminal seems to disappear, not behind his deeds but within a multi-faceted system of reference that goes back to the various phases of his development.

Anyone who attempts to interpret human beings' gestures, statements, deeds and dreams starts from the premise that every person is familiar with himself but also remains partly a stranger to himself. Not because he disguises himself in order to appear different from what he really is, but because he himself does not know what he is. He resembles a person who can pronounce perfectly many words in a foreign language but only knows the meaning of a few of them and is not even sure of those.

These few remarks on methods and concepts may help explain why psychology should in fact be regarded as a discipline of dissolution that is only partially a science; it is also a philosophy and perhaps primarily an art. In psychology it is not sufficient to trace the correct connection between cause and effect; understanding must be added, so that a given state of affairs can be interpreted, not merely explained. All knowledge of human nature depends on both knowledge and understanding, which together lead to interpretation.

The Delphic command "Know thyself," seemingly so trivial, is a huge demand born of profound doubt. Admitting the necessity that one know oneself constitutes an admission of one's own ignorance. But how does a person who has lived happily in harmony and confidence suddenly catch himself in the act of concealing parts of himself from himself? In the Oracle's demand one might see an allusion to a split consciousness. But does Apollo order a wave to come up on the shore and observe and know itself when he knows that it would disappear in the process?

Is a person who has seen into himself the same person he set out to find? Yes and no. He is the same in that part of himself which he has snatched from the jaws of the unknown. In order to succeed in such a venture, a man must go through a special crisis, in the course of which he risks becoming a stranger to himself; after overcoming the crisis he finds his way back via new insights to himself.

The estrangement results from a surprising and sometimes shocking discovery; he knows that he is still the same person, yet he finds out that he is also different from the person he had always considered himself identical with. The parallel would be the situation of a man who looks in the mirror after a long illness and sees a face that he knows belongs to him, but which he would take for a stranger's if he did not know better.

A piece of the iceberg has surfaced—it is not really new, since it has always been there. In order for us to experience this sort of thing, we must switch off our automatisms for a while. As in every serious crisis, our gestures and words, our standard strategems and habitual actions and reactions fail. It is unlikely that anyone becomes a psychologist before going through such crises and overcoming them. The experience enables him to see himself in a totally new light, to place things, actions, events and experiences in a context that is truly appropriate to them. He must find a total correlation between the basis of his character and his life-goals or purposes; it is a particular way of linking cause and effect. The important thing is to separate the innumerable *possible* circumstances from the *likely* ones, and to separate among these the determining ones from the merely conditioning ones. One might think that the process of interpretation would present incredible difficulties. But long before there were computers and other mechanical means to simplify the understanding and prediction of developments, certain individuals had already given proof of their sound grasp of past and future events. Such understanding has existed for thousands of years in philosophy, in literature, and in the artistic creations of almost all cultures.

To attain this understanding one must push one's own likes and dislikes, hopes and fears, aside. A rabbi once complained that although the hand is only a small part of the body, hardly visible in the universe, it can shut out the whole world when it covers our eyes. We are more than a hand; we often get in our own way. In order to look at a person and be able to perceive and understand him, one must be able to get out of one's own line of vision.

Self-forgetfulness is never total—we cannot avoid including ourselves in every judgment we pass on another person. We smuggle ourselves into every picture we paint of someone else. We give the other person features that are borrowed from ourselves, or—what amounts to the same thing—we distort those features in such a way that they are extremely different from ours, the very opposite. One can constantly stumble over oneself and still not fall, continuing to hobble clumsily but persistently toward one's goal. That is the usual gait of psychologists.

But—to return to my original question—why does a person become a psychologist? Is it the overwhelming desire to understand others, the result of fellow-feeling, an act of solidarity with one's own kind? It is all that, and something else besides. We must consider several seemingly contradictory interpretations at once, before we find the explanation that reconciles them. One must know oneself, we said, in order to overcome a crisis, in order to become another person, when one no longer wants to be the person one used to be. Perhaps the same sort of self-conquest is involved here as in understanding another person—perhaps.

According to certain concepts in magic and religion, one can exercise power over other beings if one discovers their names. Magicians and priests claim to know the true names of spirits and gods and thus to have a certain influence over their decisions. Rumpelstiltskin thinks that one cannot hurt him as long as no one knows that he is called Rumpelstiltskin. Knowledge of another person, of his past and of his dreams for the future, can be used as a weapon against him. Someone who understands, not merely knows, may experience the intoxication of power; but that is rarer than the discovery that his understanding helps him place his own existence on firmer foundations and broaden it. Nietzsche spoke not only of the will-to-power but also of self-expansion.

Does one become a psychologist out of the desire for self-expansion, for superiority over others, for power? One should be careful not to answer with a generalization; but neither should one disregard the doubts on this score that assail every true psychologist and in fact must assail him time and time again.

Chapter I

A CERTAIN DOCTOR liked to relate an episode from his
early childhood which he thought illuminated an important aspect of his character. As a six-year-old boy he
had been gripped with a horrible fear on the way to and
from school because he could not avoid going past a cemetery. This fear became all the more unbearable when he
saw that other children who took the very same route remained fearless and uninhibited. One day he decided on a
daring method. He came earlier than usual and forced himself to climb back and forth over the cemetery wall. In
this way he rid himself of his fear.

Now as coincidence would have it, the doctor met an
old schoolmate who had lived in the neighborhood and had
taken the same path to school. The doctor reminded him of
the cemetery and of his own fear of it, but was met with
total incomprehension. The old schoolmate, a perfectly reliable witness, informed him that this cemetery had never
existed and that this memory, to which the doctor so often
and so persistently reverted, was based on an occurrence
which he had fabricated, not experienced. Before the doctor would believe this explanation, he returned to the spot,

where he was forced to concede that his heroic deed had in fact been mere fantasy.

The victim of this self-deception was a psychologist whose fame rested partially on his convincing explanation of the significance and the characterological implications of early childhood recollections—Alfred Adler. He continued to relate this untrue story to his friends and students chiefly in order to append the instructive epilogue, for from this self-deception he drew a multitude of conclusions.

Alfred Adler, the second of six children, was born into a petty bourgeois Jewish family on February 7, 1870. The Adlers lived in Rudolfsheim on the outskirts of Vienna. Alfred was sickly as a child. The doctor, who was constantly coming to the house, seemed a most important person to him. Alfred was three years old when his younger brother died. A clearly genuine childhood recollection which Adler recounted to me in a private conversation in 1926, fifty-three years later, is connected with this event:

"My mother fetched me after the funeral to take me home. She was very sad and tearful but smiled a little when my grandfather, in order to comfort her, uttered a few lighthearted words which probably hinted at the possibility that more children might bless her marriage. For a long time I could not forgive my mother for that smile, and I may conclude from my anger that I was conscious, yes, very conscious of the horror of death."

At age five Adler contracted a severe case of pneumonia. Overhearing bits and snatches of a conversation between the concerned doctor and his father, the child gathered that he was going to die. Fear of death seized him. When he recovered, he knew that he would have to become a doctor.

His primary motivation was doubtless the belief that a doctor would be better protected against death. A second, less self-centered motive must have formed quite early: the desire to stand by his family and preserve them from pain and death. However, it is indubitable that the fantasy element in this childhood choice of a profession is joined by a yearning for importance, even power. One finds the same unconscious longings in children who plan to become policemen, firemen, nurses, teachers and the like. Additionally one must consider that in contrast to most others upon whom one calls for service, the doctor is materially and socially in a class far above most of his clients. A lower-middle-class child who wishes to assume this profession betrays a desire to raise himself above his milieu.

For a long time Adler remained a poor student. It took quite a while before he had made sufficient progress for his father to feel that it would make sense to send him to the university. Adler liked to describe a turning point in his school career: he was particularly weak in mathematics, but on one occasion he distinguished himself. There was a problem with which the teacher himself was having difficulty. Adler raised his hand, only to be greeted by the derisive laughter of his schoolmates and an indulgent smile from the teacher. In actuality he did not solve the problem, but he did demonstrate that it was improperly worded and thus insoluble. His success was a breakthrough. From that day forward he was an excellent mathematician, for a time the best in his class.

Adler often quoted biographical experiences which suggested that sensational turnabouts can and do occur—that a timid hare can suddenly display the boldness of a lion. He was by no means a believer in miracles, but whenever he cited these turnabouts it was in the firm conviction that every man has at his disposal much greater potentialities and capabilities that he knows.

There was one source of satisfaction in Adler's childhood: even as a small child he was unusually musical. Thanks to his good ear he was able to capture the ballads, folksongs and popular tunes which filled the Vienna air. One of his earliest recollections is based on a couplet drawn from a musical farce: a woman is mocked for brashly throwing flowerpots at her husband's head, although she claims her soul is so delicate that she cannot eat chicken. It is possible that as a child Adler brooded over this contradiction, and like his consternation at his bereaved mother's smile, it indicates that he early discovered the antithetical behavior of the world around him.

Adler was granted his Ph.D. in 1895. He began by specializing in ophthalmology but almost immediately changed to internal medicine. In 1898 he published a book entitled *Medical Handbook for the Tailoring Trade* (never translated into English). In this first work he tried to show "the relationship between the economic conditions and the ailments of a specific trade and to point out the threats to the general health that spring from a low standard of living. Such an approach, which examines the person *not as an isolated being but as a product of society*, can no longer be ignored by the medical profession."

Several years before the appearance of this book, Adler had joined the League of Socialist Students and had rapidly become one of its most prominent members. In this period he certainly read the major Marxist literature, perhaps even studied it. In addition to the *Communist Manifesto* he was acquainted with the *Critique of Political Economy* as well as the early philosophical works, including those on which Marx collaborated with Engels.

Adler showed a keen interest in the debates which brought the socialist leaders together and drove them apart. He read the works of August Bebel, Karl Kautsky, Wilhelm Liebknecht, Franz Mehring, Eduard Bernstein, Viktor Adler and others. But not until he had established his own doctrine could one have called him a Marxist. It will become increasingly apparent how much Adler's comparative individual psychology is dialectical in spirit and in form, as well as in content, and to what degree his conception of the relationship between man and the community corresponds both to the aims of the workers' emancipation movement and to the basic principles and methods of Marxism. Marx's critique of Feuerbach, especially as it was presented in the famous theses on that philosopher, contains a multitude of brilliant, challenging formulations which are certain to have impressed and influenced young Adler. He read there, among other things:

But the human essence is no abstraction inherent in each single individual. In its reality it is the ensemble of the social relations.[1]

In these same "Theses on Feuerbach" Marx states that the individual is not only the product but also the producer of his condition; he stresses vigorously that the educator must also be educated. These two fundamental dialectical tenets would form an integral part of individual psychology, although in this connection Adler was to quote neither Marx nor Engels. (In our early conversations—I had come to know him through his interest in a paper I had written in 1921 entitled "On the Psychology of the Revolutionary"— he quoted both Marx and his disciples quite often.)

When in 1898 Adler demanded that the doctor should examine his patient "not as an isolated being but as a product of society," he had without realizing it entered the realm of psychology. Marxism, the idea of a social hygiene principally devoted to workingmen, and critical reexamination of traditional concepts of illness all drove Adler toward psychology. His ideas on the subject crystallized a few years later while he was doing research for his *Study of Organ Inferiority*, which he submitted— unsuccessfully —as his post-doctoral dissertation. In the preface to this, his first important work, which appeared in 1907, he states:

Moreover it was for me an exciting challenge to see the ossified, limited concept of illness in complete dissolution, to be able to observe human pathology in flux.

Adler's concept of illness read:

Illness results from inferior organs and exterior strain.

He defines the inferior organ as

a malformed organ which is retarded in its development and whose growth is entirely or partially arrested.[2]

Adler's objective was to prove that two equally inferior organs can vary greatly in their capacity for performance. It thus became necessary to ask what importance mental factors have for the augmentation or diminution of performance by so-called normal organs but particularly by inferior organs. Questions about the myriad links between the mind and organ function were by no means new. They had escaped neither magicians nor priests, neither the philosophers nor alert doctors. Adler presented the issue anew, proceeding from the premise which the demonstrable presence of inferior organs in every human organism seemed to suggest.

In a lecture delivered the same year (1907) before the Philosophical Society of the University of Vienna, Adler summarized his insights as follows:

> The inferior organ needs a longer time to return to normal functioning and in the process experiences a number of disorders which can only be overcome by increased brain performance.
>
> Mental and emotional difficulties correspond to organically impeded adaptation to life. The battle to overcome these difficulties results in certain psychic attitudes and noticeably unique character traits. Here one can pinpoint the transition from physical to psychic phenomena.
>
> The outcome of overcompensation depends on several factors. One such factor familiar to us is the structure of society, the individual's social interest.[3]

The inferiority complex, an expression which was quickly to become famous and to make Adler himself famous, was frequently and improperly understood to be an extension and a mental reflection of inferior organs. This error was soon recognized even by laymen, for we all know that feelings of inferiority are not attributable to inadequate organs alone. All the more so as such peculiarities in many cases go unnoticed and therefore unacknowledged. Most people preserve long after childhood an amazing ignorance about their own bodies. So long as pain does not impel them to self-discovery, they take their bodies for granted. (Bodily peculiarities, on the other hand, often imbue children with the notion that they are special, either superior or inferior, even when neither presumption has any foundation.)

It is the fate of man to be fully conscious of his own inferiority; yet he may interpret it in any number of ways:

he can believe himself condemned to eternal inferiority and accordingly give up hope, or he can place his faith in the future and dismiss the present. His attitude is the result of a multidimensional process that includes all manner of insights and objectives, achieving unpredictable and, so to speak, illogical results. Contrary to a widespread notion, the demonstrable existence of feelings of inferiority means very little. In the first place, everyone has them; in the second place, what matters is how the individual copes with them, what he does to combat them, what he plans to make of them.

Under the influence of his teacher Brücke and the materialist ideas of the physiologists Du Bois-Reymond and Helmholtz, Sigmund Freud tried to establish a physiology of the mind. Almost against his will he arrived at a psychology which he could accept only if it were scientific, that is, if he could discover physiological laws expressed in concrete psychic form, and if they could be confirmed by the methods of natural science. From about 1898 on, Alfred Adler had been looking for evidence that would make it possible to study the sick or the healthy human being, not only as psycho-physical entity, but also as a complex of social conditions. It never occurred to him—any more than it did to Freud—to give up medicine for psychology. He wanted to study within his own field those social factors that affect psychic and physical states or perhaps dictate them completely. He hoped his findings would lead to the formation of a social medicine. Thus Adler came rather late to his calling. After completion of his studies he continued to attend lectures and seminars on psychiatry, particularly those held in the clinic of the world-famous Krafft-Ebing, whose works always appealed to him. But nothing could induce him to become a psychiatrist or a

neurologist himself. Nor did he consider devoting himself
to psychological research. The practical knowledge of human nature employed in dealing with patients continued to
interest him; it was second nature to him, for in his contacts with his own patients and their families he resorted
to it daily.

Between 1902 and 1908 Freud undoubtedly played an
important role in Adler's life. The difference between this
relationship and that between Dr. Breuer and Freud is
marked. Dr. Joseph Breuer was for many years a helpful
friend to his younger colleague and remained so until
Freud brought about a still unexplained break. Thanks to
his extraordinary gifts of observation, Breuer had discovered and first applied the cathartic method of treating
hysteria. This he accomplished without prior knowledge
of the teachings of certain psychiatrists of the Paris and
Nancy schools (Charcot, Bernheim, Liebault and Janet).
Under his influence Freud dedicated his first psycho-patho-
logical studies to hysteria. These were to estrange Freud
from his supervisor, the highly respected Professor Mey-
nert, and even more from his colleague. Dr. Breuer himself
showed little interest in his own discovery. Unlike his pupils
and collaborators, he apparently hardly suspected what unusual perspectives his work had opened up.

When Adler first heard Freud speak on his views—that
would have been in 1899 or 1900 at the Vienna Medical
Association—the *Interpretation of Dreams* had already appeared. It was a work brilliant in its originality, audacious
in concept and inexhaustible in allusion and supposition.
Adler must have been familiar with this work even though
"not a leaf . . . stirred to show that the interpretation of
dreams meant anything to anyone. . . . The book's recep-
tion, and the silence since, have once more destroyed any

budding relationship with my environment," as Freud wrote in a letter to his friend Wilhelm Fliess.[4] The founder of psychoanalysis met with extraordinary, often insulting opposition. Those enemies who did not simply hush up the issue usually refused to engage in substantive discussion. They preferred to make the inconvenient revolutionary ridiculous, spreading unflattering suspicions about him in the hope of destroying at the very outset all serious interest in his ideas. Freud met with open hostility and cutting ridicule when he lectured before the Medical Association. Adler, a witness to these proceedings, was appalled, and expressed his feelings publicly in a medical journal, giving an exhaustive account of Freud's lecture. He demanded that Freud and his teachings be given the attention they deserved. Freud sent his thanks to Adler with word that he considered Adler's piece on him the best such article that had appeared yet. This contact led to the first meeting between these two very dissimilar men.

To better understand the revealing development of a relationship which proved so significant for the history of interpretive psychology, one should examine the particular situation of these two doctors and of their country, and try to form a picture of the intellectual, moral, and cultural climate they were working in.

As I said earlier, neither Adler nor Freud had intended originally to become a psychologist or psycho-pathologist. Since their initial positions were as different as their characters, one cannot help wondering whether some common factor did not exist that affected both men similarly. They were both Austrians—and at the turn of the century that indicated much more than a common nationality. In addition to this they both came from petty bourgeois families of limited means. And both were Jews. These last two factors were of overwhelming importance, for becoming a doctor under these circumstances would entail a rise in social status which would be accompanied by alienation from the parental milieu and possibly from the parents themselves.

Jakob Freud, Sigmund's father, had grown up in Buczacz, a little town in East Galicia under conditions which the once well-known author Karl Emil Franzos, who came from the same region, called "half Asiatic." The family came to Vienna by way of Freiberg, a small Moravian town, where Freud was born on May 6, 1856. Like many other Jewish families, they came hoping to achieve bourgeois security, prosperity and prestige. But Freud's father achieved nothing. Like Dickens' Micawber, he always expected that in the near future "something would turn up." As it happened, his wife's relatives were constantly being called upon to contribute to the family's support. So trying was this memory to Sigmund Freud that at the age of forty-three he could write, "I once knew helpless poverty and have a constant fear of it." [5] The first son of Jakob Freud's second marriage, Sigmund, whose intelligence became noticeable very early, was determined to go far in life, to leave poverty behind and to escape the existence of those hapless souls who languish in the shadow of the rich and powerful.

Anyone who came from the back alleys, as it were, had to get on without the protection which a well-situated family effortlessly procured for its offspring. A poor young Jew from the East who completed his medical studies in the Vienna of the 1880s and wanted to make a name for himself had to overcome a multitude of invisible obstacles. He had to accomplish something extraordinary

and in the process demonstrate that he was more industrious, more assiduous than the others, and, moreover, original. He always had to give the impression of being an in-
novator in his field, an inventor, a discoverer; yet he also
had to remain humble lest he arouse too much resistance.
Freud of course wanted to become a university professor.
He chose physiology because he, with quite a few of his
contemporaries, believed that this was the discipline to
which the future belonged, since it formed the basis of all
medical research. Two times he seemed within reach of
brilliant success. The second opportunity presented itself
when he began to experiment with the little-known drug
cocaine, recommending it as a harmless stimulant. Perhaps
because of his eagerness to succeed he failed to recognize
what a dangerous temptation the drug could become. He
also overlooked its usefulness for surgery, something others
would soon demonstrate.

At that time Freud was living under extreme stress and
suffered constantly from migraine headaches and other
nervous afflictions. After his error with regard to cocaine
had become obvious, the deeply disappointed young doctor
wrote his fiancée and future wife that from now on he
wanted to be just as humble in the conduct of his work
as the *goyim* "and not chase after any discoveries or try
to plumb unknown depths."

It is worth mentioning that the imperial Minister of
Education was finally persuaded to confer the title of
professor upon the no longer young Jewish *Privatdozent*.
Freud received the title only because a woman of society
brought forward a whole battery of arguments to convince
the Minister of Freud's merits. The crucial argument was
probably this enthusiastic disciple's promise that when
Freud had been made professor she would donate a paint-

ing which the Minister greatly admired to the National
Museum; this she did. The painting, which probably still
hangs somewhere in an Austrian museum, was a highly
prized work by the fantastically popular Swiss painter
Arnold Böcklin. It honestly deserves its name of "Castle
Ruins."

Freud, throughout his life, was consciously a Jew.
He never tried to conceal, let alone deny, his origins.
Though he often said that he hated Vienna with all his
heart, and felt liberated whenever he left his native city,
it was a city to which he remained hopelessly tied. Thus
his Jewish sense of identity was kept intact, which meant
among other things that it did not provide a source of
feelings of inferiority—although it did cause him considerable personal difficulties. Freud was not Judeocentric,
but he did believe that he could only rely on Jewish
friends and collaborators. The exception that proves this
rule is the fact that for many years he eagerly cultivated
the friendship of Carl Gustav Jung and got him elected
the official representative of the international psychoanalytical movement. It is also not surprising that, to his
and their sorrow, he broke with his most intimate friends,
intransigently, in Old Testament style, a wrathful god who
usually contrived to conceal his wrath in such a way as to
appear reluctant but who cleverly induced his disciples to
hunt down and destroy his quarry, the friend who had
fallen from grace for apparently betraying him. The tiniest
friction, the mere hint of a difference of opinion would
suffice to make Freud lose faith in an old friendship, which
he would then renounce and liquidate.

This propensity was certainly connected with his Jewishness and his overalert fear of hostility of his Christian
environment—but only in that a fundamentally neurotic

attitude could be socially legitimized (and thus easily "rationalized") because of a specific nonpersonal situation, namely the situation of the Jew. Freud explained the characteristic aspects of his behavior thus:

My emotional life has always insisted that I should have an intimate friend and a hated enemy. I have always been able to provide myself afresh with both, and it has not infrequently happened that the ideal situation of childhood has been so completely reproduced that friend and enemy have come together in a single individual. . . .[6]

In a letter to his friend Wilhelm Fliess, Freud traced this attitude back to his relationship to a nephew, one year his senior, and to his younger brother. They "determined, not only the neurotic side of all my friendships, but also their depth." [7]

One might conclude that Freud's love-hate disposition was sufficiently motivated even without his being Jewish, on the basis of his individual psychological makeup. Yet one must not overlook the fact that he found himself in a very difficult position when, as he reported, "announcement of my unpleasing discoveries had as its result the severance of the greater part of my human contacts." [8] With the bitter self-irony which one finds more often in Jewish intellectuals than in others, he had to admit to himself that he was now, so to speak, doubly Jewish, because in addition to the fate implied by his birth he was now suffering another characteristically Jewish fate—and this he had brought on himself by his own best efforts. Twice as isolated as before, attacked by many, ridiculed by his detractors, who made it a point of pride not to read his works—his was the centuries-old experience of Jewish men on Christian territory.

In 1926, on the occasion of his seventieth birthday, Freud spoke before the B'nai B'rith Association, describing his difficult beginnings. He admitted:

I felt as though I were despised and universally shunned. In my loneliness I was seized with a longing to find a circle of picked men of high character who would receive me in a friendly spirit in spite of my temerity. Your society was pointed out to me as the place where such men were to be found.[9]

In point of fact Freud remained faithful to this Jewish lodge until the end of his life and persuaded his best friends to join it.

Freud's father came from an area where religious belief dominated men's hearts and souls, determined every detail of daily life, and at the same time demanded that intellectual acuity that finds expression in the wisdom of the Talmudists and the mysticism of the Hasidim, as well as in self-mocking humor. Adler's father, on the other hand, came from the Burgenland, from a small village with next to no Jewish culture. To be sure, the Jewish holidays were observed in his house—on feast days and perhaps on the Sabbath young Alfred went to the synagogue—but in the Adler household there prevailed a pallid, watered-down version of Judaism. Adler remembered this or that occurrence connected with religious observances, an incident in the synagogue or an episode during Passover, but these recollections were oddly lacking in substance and in part distorted by ignorance. He remembered, for example, that on the evening of Passah an angel had been awaited, and he had been skeptical about the whole thing. In actuality the family had been waiting—without real faith but following tradition—for the prophet Elijah to appear.

Freud's family lived in the Vienna Leopoldstadt, a Jewish neighborhood. The Adlers lived in an outlying district, where there were few Jews, so that young Alfred had almost exclusively Christian playmates. They probably did not even know that he was Jewish, for Adler did not fit the image of the typical Jew. For that reason he seldom or never had the unpleasant experiences which could hardly be avoided in Vienna, where anti-Semitic rowdyism was widespread. Perhaps it was never brought home to Adler that he was different, inferior to the people in the streets, the so-called "true Viennese."

Adler liked to refer back to his days as a street urchin. Although he was a sickly child, he spent almost all of his free time "in the streets," a place, he always said, especially suited to a child's self-education, a place to learn certain forms of social behavior and to practice them. This is where you have to take sides, face the music, prove that you can stick by your friends. Any sign of cowardice is punished almost instantaneously. In these street-urchin days Adler developed his group consciousness. In contrast to Freud, he felt from the first that he belonged, and in no way did he feel himself to be foreign, an unwanted addition. He considered himself a member of the community, a community which must have appeared to him the natural and only possible one. If one does not bear in mind this sense of belonging, Adler remains uncomprehensible, for he had a tendency which became more insistent with the passing years to emphasize the importance of the community and the emotions and actions inspired by it.

Yet this very insistence makes one wonder: did group-consciousness exercise such a strong influence over Adler that he easily overlooked the actual differentness of his family, of its faith and of its traditions? Did he consider these differences so slight that he was able to disregard them, refusing to let them diminish his allegiance to the outside world?

At least one argument speaks both for and against this postulation: as a young man Adler had himself baptized. He did not take this step under the influence of the Catholic Church, whose ubiquity and power could be perceived everywhere in those days. And the attractiveness of the Protestantism he adopted was by no means irresistible. For Adler was decidedly unbelieving, totally without faith. During the years I knew him I was convinced that Adler was far and away the most radical atheist I had ever met. He seemed to lack all grasp of the value of faith, which to me—then as now a confirmed atheist—seemed obvious. But let me mention here that in Adler's later works another position emerges: a willingness to understand, perhaps even an inclination to believe.

Why did the socialist freethinker have himself baptized? Quitting the Jewish congregation would have sufficed to show that he was a freethinker—no longer belonging to the faith into which he had been born and in no way obligated to it. The baptism of a nonbeliever was something else: an escape from Judaism. In going over to the Protestant faith Adler hoped to find a refuge from the peculiar fate of the Jewish community and from the consequences of his Jewish birth. This desire motivated him more strongly than one would gather from the details of his biography, most of which we owe to him.

Our private conversations, which are among my most

cherished memories, often lasted until late into the night, and there was hardly a subject of consequence upon which we did not touch. At the time I thought Adler placed utmost trust in me. It is more than probable that I did right to think so. In spite of this, one issue remained unmentioned in our conversations: the Jewish question. I had learned quite by chance about his baptism, which lay many years in the past. It came as a deeply disappointing revelation; I did not want to think about it and never broached the subject, not least of all because I knew Adler had not taken this symbolic step for the sake of a new belief. Like every Jew of my persuasion, I had no objection to a genuine conversion—that is, a conversion prompted by belief; but I was inclined to detest those who became Christians out of opportunism.

But was Adler an opportunist? I would be as hesitant to call him that now as I was then. His baptism can be explained first by the fact that he could not come to terms with being a Jew; his Jewishness had become an emotional burden to him which he could not throw off. Perhaps he found this the case because he lived in Vienna, the capital of anti-Semitism. And second, he had a logical and perfectly adequate reason: it was ridiculous that he and his descendants should suffer for a religion to which nothing bound him and whose precepts he did not observe. Why make a meaningless sacrifice when one could escape once and for all the effects of an accident of birth? Finally, Adler had a positive reason. If asked what he was first and foremost, Adler had since childhood been able to answer honestly, "a Viennese." A Viennese, not necessarily an Austrian and certainly not a Jew. This meant that in line with his sense of community it might not be essential to belong to the same church, but one did have to belong officially to the religion of the overwhelming, or we might say, overbearing majority of Viennese.

Freud must have early found out that Adler had been baptized. I have no knowledge that he ever mentioned it, although for obvious reasons he might have done so in the lodge or among very close friends. At any event, Adler's conversion to Christianity might have been an additional ground for Freud to withhold full trust from this colleague. It is probable that he regarded the baptism as a betrayal motivated by ambition and opportunism, and judged it accordingly.

Adler's speech—the accent of the suburbs which remained discernible even when he spoke academic German —this natural, unabashed Viennese *patois*, had its appeal. And although it certainly would not have offended Freud if he had heard it from someone answering to the name of Zeichenberger or Novotny, in Adler, "a Jewish kid from the suburbs," it served to remind Freud of how different was Adler's Jewishness from his.

Chapter II

I N SPITE OF his extraordinary acumen and alertness, Freud, the most famous psychologist the world has ever known, was a poor judge of human nature. Yet he knew exactly how to judge a person's intellectual abilities, so long as he was not blinded by his own prejudices.

After the first meeting with Adler, Freud realized that he had found a very intelligent, perceptive and intuitive colleague who was as interested as he was, though for other reasons, in psychopathology, particularly in the connection between physical and psychic phenomena. He offered Adler help and encouragement and gave him just that. He sent patients to him and made him known in his own circles. But Adler was never to belong to Freud's most intimate friends; he was neither a card partner nor a lodge brother, and relations between the two families were never established.

Freud must have made a deep impression on everyone with whom he had dealings in those days. There is a special aura surrounding a person whose formidable intellectual accomplishments have been denied recognition and success. A particular pathos moves all who see an injustice being perpetrated on a scale as large as the man's gifts and accomplishments, and for that reason the circle around Freud publicly .proclaimed its loyalty to the misunderstood, often insulted researcher and rallied around him, defying those who did not know and—worst of all—did not want to know what it was all about. Some of these followers believed, with Freud, that above and beyond the question of race and religion he had once again encountered a typically Jewish situation. Although similar situations arise in all groups—whether Jewish or not—which coalesce around misunderstood philosophers, artists, scholars or inventors, in this particular case those involved were almost exclusively Jewish intellectuals, mostly younger doctors for whom this special condition was merely a new variant of the familiar Jewish experience.

By no means all of those who came to discuss neuropsychology at Freud's apartment on Wednesday evenings considered themselves Freud's pupils or psychoanalysts according to the still rather fuzzy definition of the day. Most of the participants, it is true, were indebted to Freud in more ways than one; many of them adhered to him faithfully and were willing to follow loyally wherever he might lead. Adler could not be such an unconditionally dedicated disciple. His personal relationship to Freud demanded neither practical nor emotional dependency of this kind. Moreover, Adler was opposed at the time to any form of orthodoxy. Finally, and most significantly, there was from the very outset a wall separating the two men, although neither of them was really conscious of it.

Freud had begun by studying the family, particularly the secrets of its bedrooms and nurseries. In later years he would reduce national history, indeed human history, to the *chronique scandaleuse* which was dictated, endlessly repeated, and imperfectly repressed by the Oedipus complex. Adler, for his part, did not fail to recognize the significance of the complex relations existing within the family and their lasting effect on all concerned. His contribution to the analysis of these relations represents one of the most meaningful achievements of his individual psychology. Still, Adler considered the family only part of the total community. The unitary approach, without which no emotional occurrence, no impulse, no deed is explicable, always has the relation of the individual to society as its focal point. Influenced by childhood experiences, and doubtless also by Marxism and the proletarian emancipation movement, Adler saw the family as a changeable communal form, whose significance and function would have to be analyzed in terms of society, to the benefit of psychology as well. His two starting points— in 1890 as well as in 1902 and thereafter—were always the same: the somatic on the one hand, particularly as it related to the role of inferior organs, and the social on the other, especially critical analysis of the prevailing antagonistic social order.

Freud, Adler and the representatives of almost all the schools of analytical psychology refused to accept the idea of psychic heredity, or rather, to attribute much importance to it for the development of the personality. It is all the more revealing that Freud made an exception for the Oedipus complex; he saw it not only as ontogenetically unavoidable, but also phylogenetically inherent and thus as inherited. Adler for his part applied the very same supposition to his concept of social interest (*Gemeinschaftsgefühl*). Jung went the furthest in this regard, but the uninterrupted life of the "collective unconscious" in no way contradicts his basic theory; in fact it is a basic precondition.

Even before the rupture between Freud and Adler in 1911, other far-reaching differences had begun to emerge. Sooner or later they would have to drive these men apart. As I said, Freud had started out by looking for a physiology of the psyche. Over the course of many years he made every effort to define his discoveries as mechanisms and to describe how they functioned. He remained convinced that scientific certainty with regard to psychic phenomena could only be achieved if these phenomena could be recognized, described, examined and analyzed as mechanisms. The younger generation to which Adler belonged was more heavily influenced by philosophers and sociologists and no longer believed that the sciences dealing with man —Friedrich Engels called them historical, others called them the "moral sciences"—necessarily had to adopt or imitate the methods of the natural sciences. Adler replaced the mechanism with something which could be designated by a word which is nowadays extremely popular and often misused: the model. Just as Marxism defines history as— among other things—a succession of societal forms, just as it establishes models which are differentiated according to the prevailing relations of production and the corresponding class relationships, so Adler was tempted to set up analytical models of behavior in place of mechanisms and personality types. He never referred to them in this precise way, speaking instead of leitmotifs which determined the actual individual model, and which he called *individual life style*.

This term is indicative of an unimportant but disturbing weakness in the founder of individual psychology: with rare exceptions, he described his findings in everyday words instead of inventing special terms. This is one reason why his originality has almost never been seen in its proper light and why his ideas have been recognized and acknowledged only to a limited extent.

To return to the break between Freud and Adler: certain character traits were largely to blame. Adler, who was fourteen years younger than Freud, could not accept him as a fatherly authority. It would have seemed more natural to regard him as an older brother. But Adler was a second-born child who had always assumed a hostile, combative attitude toward the first-born. As mentioned above, Freud was inclined to see his younger brother as his most intimate friend and archrival, so that "friend and enemy have come together in a single individual." One may be allowed to generalize that Freud's closest and most faithful friends and disciples were men who in their adoration and love assumed the role of younger brothers and desired nothing more than to become his apostles. Each break between one of them and the master can be attributed to qualities in the individual, but in every case Freud's characteristic pattern played an essential part.

Aside from the questions of character, there were also special grounds for Freud's bitter estrangements from this first generation of psychoanalysts: his mania for originality, and his determination to maintain his priority rights. One has to realize that in that period natural scientists were constantly uncovering new knowledge, and that these discoveries and inventions brought their authors recognition, fame and sometimes even wealth. The scientist and the technician imbued with originality were like the conquerors of new worlds, conquistadors—and it had always been Freud's burning desire to become a conquistador; even later in his career he liked to regard himself as such.

So the intellectuals who gathered around Freud were likewise under pressure to be original. They remained aloof from the official academic world of science and quite involuntarily found they had all the prominent scientists against them. They were in the precarious position of insurgents whose goals have been revealed long before they have the means to begin their struggle for power or to protect themselves against the preventive strikes of the alerted rulers. In such situations one places undue hopes in the future and demands of one's companions absolute faith in the fulfillment of these hopes.

Hardly a Wednesday evening passed when one of the participants in Freud's discussion group did not bring forth an idea which he wanted to have acknowledged as proof of his brilliance and originality. Usually he was ready with special technical terms which thenceforth were supposed to denote his finding, his discovery or his particularly ingenious interpretation. Freud could accept all this up to a point. But either during the meeting, or later, in private conversation, he would let fall that the young man's idea was actually nothing new, since he, Freud, had hit upon the same fact earlier and had merely used different terminology.

Freud experts know countless examples of such behavior, which manifested itself early when Freud abruptly terminated his close friendship with the Berlin doctor Wilhelm Fliess. Freud's mania for originality was truly excessive—and all the more amazing because Freud was in fact an original thinker from his youth and remained one until his death. Anyone who studies the history of psychoanalysis in all its ramifications is always struck by the way this curious hyperbolic weakness of Freud's spread beyond the pointless conflicts it bred and infected others as if by contagion. It is a disconcerting fact that virtually none of Freud's apostles and few of his pupils remained immune to this mania.

It was not only a question of Freud's wanting to reserve priority rights for himself; in almost all cases of disagreement Freud also had a serious and legitimate worry: the fear that his doctrine would be contaminated. Accordingly he frustrated every attempt to modify it or to make it more palatable by softening it. In actual fact, his was the severity that can scarcely be avoided in a fortress under enemy siege.

As early as 1904, Adler began to gain the impression that he did not really fit in, simply because he could not fulfill Freud's unspoken demand for complete agreement. Adler wrote Freud that he would no longer participate in the evening discussion groups. Freud, however, wanted him to stay on and knew exactly how to get him to revoke his decision. Shortly after sending his letter Adler, through Freud's efforts, was made chairman of the Vienna Psychoanalytic Association.

In a few areas Freud and Adler were certainly of one mind, and Adler could perhaps consider himself Freud's disciple: in their studies on hysteria Freud and Breuer had formulated a psychogenetic interpretation of neurotic disorders. Adler also shared Freud's view on the role of the unconscious and, I believe, on repression. Although the individual psychology Adler formulated does not attribute any special importance to repression, it remains true that long after the break Adler tended to view repression as a significant psychic phenomenon. And there are other details of Freudian psychoanalytic theory to which Adler ascribed great meaning during his years of working with Freud, and even later, such as the significance assigned to

dreams and their interpretation in the treatment of psycho-
neuroses, although Adler did not subscribe to Freud's
system of dream interpretation.

There is no question that Adler originally toyed with
the idea of a psychology of drives. He expected it to provide scientifically verifiable solutions to the essential problems of emotional development. Of course Adler's approach
was biological or organological, while Freud's was physiological. For Adler the drive or instinct was the most primitive, most general activation of an organ, corresponding
to the need for gratification—the libido—in Freud's system.
Libido—this word borrowed from sexology—may be vari-
ously interpreted, but at the time it was credited in the
Freudian system with being the unique psychic energy
that accounts for all activity.

No matter how valid Freud's imposing system may seem,
it loses all value unless one accepts the central position of
the libido theory that Freud insisted upon. But Adler was
one of the few in that narrow circle who even in the early
years did not adhere to or adhered only partially to this
theory. Freud strictly rejected any lukewarmness, any
compromise about the theory on Adler's part—and he was
right to do so. One can understand the controversy better
when one realizes that it revolved around the issue which
occasioned the greatest opposition to Freud even after
World War I: the question of sexuality and its part in
the evolution of the psyche. Neither Adler nor the other
members of the circle who were to break with Freud in
1911 dreamt of abandoning their inquiries into sexuality—
a factor which had been deliberately underrated and obscured, due to prevailing moral objections. They realized
on the other hand that strictly speaking—that is, in accordance with Freud's own interpretation—identification of the

libido with so-called pan-sexualism (which was only one form of libido) was not justified.

But even if one recognizes all of this, the fact remains that both in psychoanalytic practice (in neurosis therapy, for instance) and in psychoanalytic theory sexuality has taken over the libido to the point that the latter is reduced to the former. Freudian analysis reveals instinctive and repressive mechanism which always add up to the same thing. Regardless of what trauma is discovered, regardless of the family situation and the personal history of the neurotic and his next of kin, the Oedipus complex in Freudian psychoanalysis is as unavoidable as death. Freud was absolutely right—and who could have been a more competent psychoanalyst than he?—the Oedipus complex is the heart of his theory of neurosis and therefore of all psychoanalysis.

Adler resisted this theory; his rejection of it became all the more resolute with the years, while the "sexualization" of psychoanalysis became more dogmatic. Unlike the enemies surrounding the besieged fortress, Adler did not doubt the importance of sexuality, but he wanted to do justice to the full range of motivations that dictate the actions and failures of human beings. Freud, in his *History of the Psychoanalytic Movement* (1914), explained this apostasy by saying that Adler held a socialist point of view which made him incapable of understanding psychoanalysis as it had to be understood. Freud presented Adler's heresy in a way calculated to frustrate Adler's efforts at obtaining an academic chair, since it could be taken for granted that the socialist leanings of a candidate would make him immediately unacceptable to many. And indeed, Adler did not get the post he had applied for at the University of Vienna.

Of course the suggestion that Marxist or socialist convictions diminish or destroy the capacity to understand psychoanalysis is patently ridiculous. Adler was perfectly well able to grasp Freud's ideas, but he ascribed the phenomena that helped make the Oedipus complex the focal point of Freud's neurosis theory to a different source, namely authoritarian society and the authoritarian behavior it spawns. This behavior intrudes upon all human relations; in ancient Rome, for example, the *pater familias* had power of life and death over all the members of the family. Adler realized that he had to start with the forms of social organization, with an analysis of the authority relationships in the state, the tribe, and the family, in the relationships among the classes, and in the relations of generations and the sexes to one another. He recognized that wherever one found man ruled by an authority one also found antagonisms, and these would invariably turn up, more or less transformed, in the psyche.

No matter what Freud claimed, the fact remained that for a good many years he and his associates had valued Adler's ability to understand psychoanalysis so highly that they had voted him the president of the Vienna Psychoanalytical Association and entrusted him with the publication of their journal.

When one follows the course of the protracted squabbles between these psychologists, one is struck by certain behavior patterns, by the distressing misconceptions which gave these confrontations a particularly unfortunate character. The orthodox psychoanalysts reproached those who broke with them—or those whom they ostracized—with never having understood what it was all about. For if they had understood what Freud taught, they would have admitted that he was absolutely right in everything. A form of combat soon developed; it employed defamatory methods and was thus particularly menacing. Freud's troops explained the schismatics' "inability to understand" as the result of unconscious resistance produced by a psychic disorder, perhaps even mental derangement. Such ad hoc diagnoses, spread by a whispering campaign, were used as secret weapons against the heretics. Combined with this were pseudo-psychological revelations about the unbridled ambition of the defectors, their passion to be recognized as founders of a school and to assume an unearned position of authority—and so on.

What took place during those days spread. It is sad but true that many victims of this process of disparagement later used the very same techniques, including the so-called diagnosis, against those who differed with or opposed them. This strategy should not be attributed solely to the character of these polemicists and their special situation; it is a natural outgrowth of every secular mysticism, as well as of every form of sectarianism.

One can assert, though it is difficult to prove, that no belief has ever disappeared without leaving traces which are assimilated, with modifications into new belief. In this sense one may predict with resignation that no belief and especially no superstition will perish completely so long as men walk the earth.

Religion offers its believers conclusive answers to basic questions about the world, life, mankind; solutions provided by older religions are on the one hand partially integrated into newer ones, on the other hand cast aside as dangerous heresies, fiendish delusions, or childish ignorance. When any religion is past its prime its answers no longer seem definitive and therefore no longer carry conviction; they no longer inspire the awe which once made them absolute. In this phase mysticism usually springs up. Regardless of the form it takes, it teaches that there are undiscovered secrets which guard and conceal the essential truths. Mysticism often remains silent on whether God chooses that these truths be kept secret or whether this peculiar game of hide-and-seek is that victory of which God cannot or will not deprive the devil—this, too, for secret reasons.

Mysticism promises to bring the undreamt-of to light and to reveal the meaning of whatever seems senseless or even nonsensical. Although every mysticism proclaims fanatical belief, sooner or later it will have to seek its triumph and fulfillment in heresy. It is not surprising that whoever snatches God's secret from Him opens the door to the devil. Wherever he turns, the mystic is surrounded by demons he himself has summoned.

After the bourgeois revolution completed its work of secularization, there came into being a worldly mysticism which embraced both philosophy and age-old superstitions. Marxism, which synthesized the eschatology of prophetic Judaism and Hegel's optimistic philosophy of history, undertook not only to reveal the secrets of history and its ultimate destiny but also to hasten its coming. The orthodox Marxist is absolutely certain that he can explain the seemingly pointless, even disgracefully absurd course of history as lucidly as he can explain current events—wars, the creation of ideologies, the progress of technology, the fall of empires, and so on. He can uncover their real meaning in terms of historical laws.

No mysticism can concede to its opponents that their opposition is compatible with knowledge of its teachings or with genuine conviction. Here once again the devil proves how useful he is: he prevents true insight; the opposition has sold out to him lock, stock and barrel; that is why it raises objections. The Marxist can assume that he who doubts the truth is acting on behalf of the capitalists, who are incapable of recognizing the facts because these run counter to their interests. We know where such an attitude has led in Stalin's Russia and elsewhere.

Psychoanalysis, too, bears some of the traits of secular mysticism. Unlike traditional psychiatry, the modern psychopathology of the Paris, Nancy and Vienna schools held that even the most confused utterances of the mentally and emotionally disturbed had a meaning which could be ascertained if one succeeded in cutting through the confusion, in unveiling the secret. One recovered the truth from the depths, hence the curious appellation "depth psychology," which is particularly cherished by the Germans.

When a patient rejects the interpretations of the therapist treating his psychoneurosis, the therapist recognizes this as neurotic resistance and brings it to the patient's attention. The resistance has the same roots as the neurosis itself. In every treatment one encounters it; its conquest by the patient is a prerequisite to cure. But what if the patient rejects an assertion or an interpretation by his therapist simply because he knows the therapist to be wrong? After all, the patient has a more intimate knowledge of his own life.

When is the therapist really wrong? Certainly not when the patient agrees with him, and certainly not when the patient withholds his approval, something which is considered negative proof that the therapist is on the right track. But *any* relationship in which one and the same individual must always be right and in which the other individual must always be wrong leads sooner or later to subjugation of the latter, to the perpetuation of totalitarianism and humiliation. During the second decade of the twentieth century, the unique circle of the Viennese interpretive psychologists unintentionally ushered in a rule of suspicion, occasioned by a totalitarian misuse of psychology that still prevails in some places to this day.

Those were the last decades in which the ruling classes of Europe enjoyed a clear conscience; it was *la belle époque*. The sufferings of the poor caused the rich no compunctions—on the contrary, they strengthened the wealthy in their conviction that they themselves must be superior, worthy of a better fate, since they received in abundance all that which was denied to others. Wealth did not need to be excused; it helped justify all privileges, even that of ignoring those strict moral precepts whose strict observance was required of "the people." Anyone in possession of even a modicum of power reserved special privileges for himself. Appearance and make-believe magnified power in the eyes of those who served it, even in the humblest positions. The rulers for their part believed in the right of the powerful to overstep those very laws whose protection was entrusted to them.

The emperor Franz Joseph was crowned at the age of eighteen and ruled for more than half a century. His belief in Divine Right remained steadfast to the last day of his eighty-six years. To his subjects, he had long been more than a monarch; he was a grandfather and an unassailable institution besides. His end would mean far more than the death of a ruler, for it would lead to something far worse than the extinction of a dynasty. Just when the peoples of the Dual Monarchy were beginning to become conscious of national identity and transforming themselves from ethnic entities into nations yearning for sovereign status, a startling fact became obvious; being an Austrian depended on this old man, more on him than on the accident of where one was born or one's ethnic origin.

One should realize that the theme of national identity —so often mentioned and so frenetically discussed today— assumed an extraordinary importance, even before the end of the nineteenth century, in Franz Joseph's monarchy. The issue was especially crucial, for obvious reasons, to the emperor's Jewish subjects in the crown lands and also in Vienna, a city to which many of them migrated during those decades, hoping to find there a new home they could not lose. In this sense the Jewish citizens of this arch-Catholic empire were the most loyal, most genuine Austrians of all. Kafka was as little a Czech as the writer Joseph Roth was a Pole, Sigmund Freud a Ukrainian, a Pole or a Moravian, Schnitzler a Hungarian. They and many like them had one identity in common, which became more dubious with each passing day: they were Austrians.

. . Does one become a psychologist because one is no longer sure of oneself and of the world around one? This is the question I asked in my introduction. The Austria of the early twentieth century was characterized by the persistent survival of the distant past and the charming, arrogant intrusion of the recent past; it was rife with superstition, not only among the Catholics but also among the Jews, who formed isolated and extremely devout communities, especially in the Slavic parts of the Dual Monarchy.

Interpretive, "destructive" psychology, antagonistic to any kind of prejudice and superstition, was at first in fact a "Jewish science," but it was no less an "Austrian science."

It was the product of a decadent civilization which had matured with absurd unevenness, so that some parts of it were, so to speak, rotting on the vine; life and death, intellectual courage and self-righteous hypocrisy, true art and shameless artificiality not only existed side by side but secretly shared a life of publicly rejected but privately longed-for promiscuity, whose theatrical character became more and more noticeable as the tragic denouement neared. "*Eh scho' wissen*"—"Y'know what I mean?"—was an expression which hardly called for a wink anymore. It hinted that everything was a farce, that fatal passion was mere infatuation, for instance. Everything was "just for fun," "a joke," and it was "the thing to do" to act as if one did not realize that. "Don't turn your back on anything" was the rallying cry—on anything, that is, except the unpleasant.

One person pretended to play along with the comedy, providing it prolifically with lines and plots: Arthur Schnitzler.[1] Another refused to play along and became the sworn enemy of the prevailing hypocritical morality which ruined love as well as art and politics. This man, one of the most eloquent of our rhetorical century, was Karl Kraus.

Schnitzler, whose early stories, as Freud himself acknowledged, anticipated the coming of psychoanalysis, and Karl Kraus, the uncompromising exposer of hypocrisy and mendacity—these two men and some of their Austrian contemporaries made several discoveries that were not so different from those made by the men who met Wednesday evenings at Freud's apartment, before they were driven apart by their own worst impulses. Because they were Austrians and Jews in a time of impending disintegration, all these men did their utmost to find out and pub-

licize what man was, what he could be, and what he had
to become. They were interested in the whole man, in his
subconscious as well as his conscious mind, in his never
perfect knowledge of self as well as in the misconception
and misunderstandings behind which he hides from himself and others; they were interested in his half-truths, in
his judgments, his prejudices, his subterfuges and his
dreams.

Like the permanent aesthetic revolution which began
around that time, bringing immediacy in place of *trompe-
l'oeil* and artistic truth in place of artificiality, the psychologists had to imbue their contemporaries with the courage
to recognize themselves, to "become what they were," as
Nietzsche would have said. They had to strip away the
façade, to accept themselves without the farce; and all this
in order that they might be capable of changing themselves.

And did the psychologists show that this could be done?
The many quarrels and feuds which nourished the flames
of hatred bore witness to the contrary.

In 1911 Adler gave three lectures on psychoanalysis
before the steadily growing circle of devotees. He stated
the points on which he agreed and disagreed with the
founder of psychoanalysis. At the time he did not foresee how rapidly the line of demarcation he had established
would become the barrier between two implacable enemies. And Freud stealthily but firmly hastened the final
break, still not suspecting that a decade later he would be
able to reply to a visitor looking for Adler that he knew
the psychologist neither personally nor by name.

During the three evenings of discussion that followed
Adler's lectures, everything seemed to be summed up by
two alternatives: the sex drive or the will-to-power. Adler,

the heretic of the group, attacked with unexpected vehemence by Freud's loyal troops, felt himself misunderstood, even intentionally so. He did not, however, view the alternatives as meaningless, merely oversimplified and therefore misleading. He knew where the others were wrong, and, moreover, he thought he knew where he was right. In truth he was only to find this out in the course of the next twenty-six years which lay between him and sudden death on an indifferent street in a distant city and a strange land.

The Neurotic Constitution (1912), Adler's *magnum opus,* is still a valuable and instructive work, but it cannot be considered a comprehensive representation of individual psychology. The world war which erupted two years later, and the momentous events that followed it, widened the scope of this man who was by then already in his late forties. Far-sighted and perceptive, he realized at fifty what the psychology he had in mind might become and what it could accomplish, and what psychologists had to strive for—until that perhaps very near future which, as Nietzsche said, "will devote itself to one thing: education."

Part Two

Chapter III

"GUESS MY RIDDLE or die!" commanded the Sphinx. And on Crete the story went: "Find the way out of the labyrinth or be eaten by the Minotaur." In countless myths, legends, fairy tales and epic poems the hero can elude death only by making the correct guess and overpowering his foe with superhuman strength or devices. Thus Oedipus becomes king of Thebes, thus does Joseph, the interpreter of dreams, reach the foot of Pharaoh's throne.

Mankind has always had to conjecture, discover, interpret, until science and technology made this necessity obsolete by—metaphorically speaking—drawing up maps of the labyrinths and turning them into tourist spots. It is astonishing that Alfred Adler, a scholarly son of the science-mad nineteenth century, reached the pinnacle of his abilities, his knowledge, his intuitions without ever ceasing to be an inveterate solver of puzzles, a conjecturer. He did not disobey the precepts of science; he simply became convinced that the natural, or unavoidable, procedure of the psychologist was this: to advance cautiously, step for step, at first without a fixed goal, often erring and

53

correcting himself, and then by chance to discover the one road which would lead him to what he sought.

What could be a better analogy than the jigsaw puzzle? The first piece is placed on the board; it comes first only by chance. But every subsequent piece must be chosen to fit effortlessly into the preceding piece. Thus one progresses, choosing and rejecting, gradually perceiving the outlines of the picture that is emerging. But often one takes apart pieces that seemed to fit well; for only later does one recognize mistakes caused by carelessness or overeagerness.

The method employed here is no less exacting than that of the chemist, who sometimes makes many false starts before discovering the structure of a substance. The "unscientific" element in "puzzle psychology" lies only ostensibly in its method, although in point of fact this method is difficult to teach and will not work for an individual who is lacking in imagination and intuition. The unscientific aspect resides in the subject under examination, for the development of the human personality follows almost the same course as the piecing together of a puzzle. It is a process of constant guessing and comparing. (Adler at times was very insistent that his doctrine should be known as *comparative* individual psychology.)

Just consider what that miracle of early childhood, of learning to speak, entails. The one living creature that for an extended period is unable to feed and protect itself (hence the myths of maternal animals, of wolves who suckle children), this instinctless being, helpless to the point of ridicule, learns to recognize words when he can barely stand upright, before he can grasp their precise meaning. He tests them by imitating them again and again. Finally the sounds and what they express combine inextricably in the child's perception and imagination. The language which connects the child with the world can be learned only through a dialectical process of adaptation in which assimilation is simultaneously creation and the discovery of meaning is simultaneously invention.

This is by no means the only puzzle we must solve in childhood, although it is certainly the most difficult. Consider the tasks of finding one's way around in time and space, of learning where one stands in relation to objects and to the gigantic creatures which surround one, of mastering their orders and prohibitions. None of this can be accomplished without continuous experimenting and interpreting. As a result, any flaw in our development assumes immeasurable importance. This most common of human adventures, the unavoidable hazard of experimenting, is accompanied, especially during childhood, by one constant activity which makes everyday life possible. That activity is learning, or, as Adler liked to say, training: training for life. Adler was the first interpretive psychologist to acknowledge the indispensability of training and to draw conclusions from the realization that the human being must learn *everything* from scratch, not merely those movements, gestures, acts and reactions that eventually become automatic. Adler insisted that it was only through training that the individual took on those specific traits, inclinations and dislikes that characterized his behavior in all areas of life. Behavior and learning therapy, much discussed nowadays as the last word in ethology, is an old friend to individual psychologists, to experts on problem children, for example. We shall return later to the multitude of techniques one can use and to the wealth of purposes such training can serve. But first it is important to examine the chief consequences which our guessing and puzzle-solving have for the formation of the conscious, the self-conscious and the subconscious mind. Although all guessing is a kind of game, it is also a deadly serious game, one which proves unsettling, threatening. The seemingly natural feeling of security often begins to waver and then gives way to a feeling of insecurity.

But what if the feeling of insecurity were the inevitable, the first and ever-recurring experience of every human being? What if it were an element of Pascal's *conditio humana*? Adler took this idea as a basic premise. His special contribution is to have insisted quite early that this feeling is absolutely intolerable and therefore gives rise to a need for security as urgent as any organic craving.

Here I venture to assert that all the premises of Adler's system are negative. The one exception is the role assigned in individual psychology to social interest. In the spirit of the Marxian axiom that it is always "the bad side which brings a movement to life, which makes history," [1] Adler uses the following four "bad sides" as his starting points:

1. Somatic or biological inferiority condemns the newborn child to a parasitic existence which lasts a decade or longer and is possible only because of the help provided by an adult or a group such as the family.

2. The innate inferiority of organs which one can detect in every individual soon creates additional, almost insurmountable, adaptational problems and an excessive concentration of attention on the organs in question or on their functioning. This worry over their functioning can become an inexhaustible source of inferiority feelings.

3. Initiation into life takes place under extremely adverse conditions. Man must, to use a metaphor, respond in a language which he does not yet recognize as such, even before he has learned to distinguish and repeat individual

words. He cannot grasp the fact that he is an *I* until he realizes that he is a *not-I*, an external reality to all other human beings. And he cannot differentiate among other human beings until he has become self-aware as an *I*. In more general terms this means that he will have to construct his means of orientation and at the same time use them. Each process depends on the other.

The child is surrounded on all sides by danger of error: he may fail to distinguish clearly between the word and what it expresses; he may transpose cause and effect; he may misinterpret the relationship between reality and imagination or dream; he may fail to perceive spatial proximity and temporal sequence. Any road may prove a detour, if not the wrong way altogether. Nevertheless most children finish this frightful obstacle race early and plant their feet firmly on the ground as soon as they have learned to learn. Learning is the most common act of compensation. The child masters this device by age three if not sooner.

4. Consciousness, the particular framework for reflecting, confirming, preserving or aggressively changing a relationship to experienced reality, personally shapes the content of that reality, distorting, underestimating or overestimating its significance. From the moment of birth, the child is forced into a relationship created and gradually transformed by the narrow little world around him. The child eventually becomes a subject and thus capable of participating actively in the relationship. As the child changes, those around him alter their behavior toward him. We shall examine in another connection whether this represents an expulsion from Paradise, a first betrayal, the initial shock of the Oedipus complex, or the beginnings of insecurity. One thing is certain: here, too, the "bad side"

manifests itself and develops consciousness in all its forms.

Biological inferiority accounts for the excessive time required for human maturation and creates many additional problems. According to Adlerian psychology, it is one of the decisive reasons, if not the decisive one, for man's being a conscious being, the only form of life that knows beforehand that it has to die, as Voltaire said. A human being who fails to attain consciousness will fail to master almost all the other forms of necessary compensation. He will belong to the human race only by virtue of his physical appearance.

Consciousness comes about through a process at once reactive and actively creative. I know of no explanation that would be completely satisfying. Without the central nervous system, without the brain, and without constant refinements in our sensory apparatus, we would be unable to store up such quantities of experience in so relatively short a time or to classify them into a system of perception which then serves us as a built-in computer for processing experimental data. According to Adler's theory, whether one perceives or not depends on a tendentious *schema of apperception*. This pattern corresponds to the individual *life-line* which becomes fixed during the same phase of life, between the ages of three and five. But is this life-line fixed consciously or unconsciously? This question leads us by the back door to one of the most difficult and important issues in interpretive psychology. We know that in the beginning this psychology—and particularly its offshoot, psychoanalysis—amazed, distressed and provoked people because it seemed to dethrone consciousness in favor of the subconscious. This was identified as the actual source of all the drives and inclinations which form the nature of an individual and preserve or destroy his emotional health. Although the subconscious is still a bone of contention between the strictly behaviorist and materialist schools, its existence is today largely taken for granted. But what is the subconscious? Where and how does one find it?

Let us look for it in the slips we make in everyday life. Mrs. A. wants to offer her guest, Mrs. B., some cake she had bought for herself. But she cannot find the key to her pantry. She racks her brains—in vain. Mrs. B. is hardly out of the house before Mrs. A.'s memory begins to function flawlessly: she finds the key at once.

The desire to deprive her guest of the treat was something she could not admit to herself. It therefore remained subconscious and could thus be fulfilled. Was the wish *forced* down into the subconscious, where things that have been forgotten are stored? What triggered this suppression of awareness? The pleasure principle prevailed, but since it operates in open opposition to the reality principle, to the demands of society and convention, the act which provided its victory had to be covered up.

Let us observe how the same effect can be achieved by different means. The woman searches desperately for the key in the presence of her guest, and finds it as soon as the friend has left. But this time let us assume that the forgetfulness and embarrassment were feigned. Mrs. A. had already decided not to sacrifice a single crumb of her cake, but she wanted to put on a show of generosity. She played her role so well that Mrs. B. had to comfort her and beg her to stop searching.

What is the difference between these two versions? In the first instance the hostess has the feeling that only her mislaying the key prevents her from behaving in the proper manner; in the second version the real goal is the same, as is the success of the maneuver. But the hostess lies knowingly. She cannot consider herself a gracious hostess who has been thwarted by bad luck. In the first case Mrs. A. is spared a guilty conscience; in the second the subconscious played no part, and a guilty conscience might interfere with Mrs. A.'s fully enjoying her cake.

A suspicion now arises: how unconscious were Mrs. A.'s intentions in the first example? Certainly there are varying degrees of consciousness. We all know the sentence, "I can't think of it at the moment." That usually means that one knows something but is unable for the moment to raise it to the level of conscious awareness. Alfred Adler did not reject Freud's theory of repression; on the contrary, he took a great interest in the examples Freud cited in his *Psychopathology of Everyday Life.* This work details many instances of slips, of forgetfulness, of mistakes in speech, of misplacing objects. Yet Adler tended with the passing years to simplify or trivialize this new mythology of the subconscious or unconscious, this important component of the new secular mysticism, psychology. His attitude disappointed many of his students. But for him it was clear that "the unconscious is simply that which we do not understand."

If we apply this axiom to our not-so-generous Mrs. A., we can establish that at the critical moment she may not have understood what kind of game she was playing with her guest and with herself. The farce succeeded precisely because she did not understand. If she had understood, she would have been forced to admit that she was selfish, petty, and greedy. In Adler's terms; awareness is a device we use to deceive ourselves, and the *device* or *stratagem* is an extremely important concept in Adlerian analytic psychology. (A related concept that applies to more complex situations is the *arrangement*.)

If human beings are asked to draw conclusions from their own behavior, they will usually find ample grounds for choosing a flattering interpretation. We may say, therefore, that we cling to the apparent or real advantages derived from noncomprehension, so long as we do not have to sacrifice this emotional comfort in order to avoid greater disadvantages. For example, one could consider a third version of the saga of the withheld cake. Mrs. A. calls up her friend and informs her that the key turned up as soon as Mrs. B. left. She then berates herself for her absent-mindedness which, since she knows some psychology, she sees as a mask for selfishness. It is as if she were admitting to a terrible crime. Mrs. B. is then forced to find kind words for her friend and to assure her that she is not selfish. Mrs. A. remains inconsolable and forces her frustrated guest to pay her exaggerated compliments, until finally it seems to be Mrs. B. who has done something wrong.

Another example, which Adler often cited, goes as follows: a very near-sighted young man loses his pince-nez while dancing. He has to bend over and finally kneel down to find them, but he moves so clumsily that he falls down and takes his partner with him. She ends up lying on the floor. While he pats the floor in search of his pince-nez he holds the girl down with one hand and a knee, thus preventing her from getting up until he himself is ready. The point of the tale is simple. Was the man conscious of his behavior or not? Are we conscious of all our acts and gestures? It was in any case more agreeable to this awkward dancer to hold the woman down on the floor and to concentrate on finding his pince-nez. An observer would surmise that as a husband this young man would dodge responsibility and refuse to acknowledge his own mistakes if marital crises occurred.

Is this banality or frivolity the sort of thing the subconscious deals in, not "deeper," considerably deeper matters? After all, Freud demonstrated what an inaccessible dungeon the subconscious is, what unspeakably terrifying secrets lodge there, and only fifty years ago his revelations made his contemporaries shudder. They also aroused outrage, and a resistance all the more stubborn because those outraged were evidently psychically unprepared to analyze their own motives. What was at issue, and what is at issue today in psychoanalysis? Is it the revelation of incestuous desires for mother, father, sister or brother? Is it discovery of unbridled jealousy which spawns death- and murder-wishes directed, not only against one's closest kin, but also against anyone whose existence or actions get in one's way? Psychoanalysis is actually concerned with the intolerable feelings of guilt that result from such desires and jealousies, with fear of punishment and of castration and the mental illnesses into which these anxieties can be transformed—like hysteria or anxiety and compulsion neuroses. But today no one is shocked by the revelations themselves, by descriptions of sexuality in children or suppositions as to the content of the subconscious. Such matters now merely provide conversational gambits for cocktail parties. Many people nowadays would ten times rather discuss their incestuous fixations or their libidinous peculiarities and difficulties than, for instance, their stinginess or their aggravation at certain personal failures, or the fact that they are bored by museums but continue to visit them, or such physical annoyances as body odor.

And indeed why should it be a deeply traumatic experience for a child to have seen his mother or father naked or to have heard this or that remark or noticed a gesture which threatened castration, though only in joke? In the highly industrialized countries several decades of technological and social upheaval, and the concomitant changes in life style, have eliminated the oppressive fiction that sex is hopelessly sinful and spiritually unclean. The theme of sexuality has become public and unavoidable, in movies, in the theater, in the mass news media. In any case, the younger generation knows few inhibitions—either ethical or ideological—in its sex life. Incestuous fixations, even sexual relations between close blood relatives, are in many cases no longer regarded as shameful, since in affluent circles such things can easily be kept a secret and cause neither anxiety nor fear of legal repercussions. It is all the more remarkable that in the downright hallucinatory, no-holds-barred pornography of our day, especially the underground press, every adolescent and perverse fantasy is depicted in lurid and minute detail—except those dealing with incestuous motives, desires and experiences.

Conscious or unconscious incestuous attachments may generally be far less prevalent than psychoanalysts originally surmised, but even so, it is probable that they occur much more infrequently and survive for a shorter time today than at the turn of the century. One of the reasons might be that in recent generations fear of the opposite sex has greatly diminished and often completely disappeared, thanks to relatively early contacts between the sexes. Where incestuous feelings do linger past childhood, one should not consider them a result of the irresistible attraction of the past; they reveal a form of cowardice that seeks a refuge from the future in established relationships. This cowardice often stands in the way of consummating the fantasy, as Adler himself was humorously aware: Once a psychoanalyst who remained friends with Adler after the latter's "defection" from Freud in 1911 came to him with a difficult and unprecedented case. For many years he had been treating an American who was now over thirty. The analyst had finally managed to make the patient aware of his hidden motives. The man accepted all of the analyst's interpretations, including of course the diagnosis of an incestuous fixation on his mother. But then the patient announced that he did in fact want to sleep with his mother. "What should I do?" the psychoanalyst asked. After an especially long drag on his cigar, Adler calmly replied, "Tell your patient that if he really wants to sleep with his mother he should go right ahead." The psychoanalyst exclaimed, "Good heavens, what will happen if he actually does it?" Thereupon Adler answered, if possible even more genially, "Come on, *he* may be crazy, but his mother isn't. Besides, the lady is probably well along in years. And what thirty-year-old man, rich and good-looking, would start an affair with an old woman unless, like Oedipus, he stood to gain a kingdom by it?"

Nowadays we no longer see the major insight, the "deeper" content of Freudian diagnosis as the revelation of incestuous secrets, but as the exposure of guilt feelings. It is important to realize that the teachings of Sigmund Freud rests upon an Old Testament-style severity, an extremely moralistic conception of man and his guilt. Freud's morality-obsessed opponents never perceived this; their misunderstanding of Freud's motives was so profound that they considered Adler the moralist. Here ignorance occasioned a colossal error, for among the ineradicable differences between these two men are their positions on morality. Adler's psychology is second only to Nietzsche's in the lack of importance it attributes to morality as a motivating force. Adler believed neither in those guilt feelings that since Freud have been greatly overstressed, nor in guilty conscience. (Let me banish at the outset a potential misunderstanding: Adler was a highly ethical man, mindful of his duty and in every respect irreproachable. He was as little immoral as Freud was. The conduct of both of these men could have served the most puritanical bourgeois as a model—unfortunately!)

To the individual psychologist, moral compunctions are usually something fabricated by the guilty in their search for additional moral benefits. A fundamental distinction between psychoanalysis and individual psychology manifests itself here, and it has anthropological implications. In the demonology of Freud's interpretation of dreams, and in psychoanalytical neurosis studies, all the cases concerned patients who concealed their own murder wishes from themselves and nevertheless suffered from oppressive guilt feelings which caused them to lose their equilibrium. As if hunted by the Furies they vainly sought refuge in self-castigation and tremulous anxiety. Today, after two world wars, several revolutions and counter-revolutions, the rise of totalitarian dictatorships, and a boom in injustice, torture and murder, the daily perpetuation of monstrous acts has been transformed into a sort of official policy carried out by office-holding criminals and countless millions of silent accomplices. Yet the total feeling of guilt has not increased one iota—on the contrary! Fear of their own ruthlessness, and of their deserved punishment, *should* be just as excruciating for those actually guilty of these crimes, if not more so, than if they merely subconsciously plotted and imagined the deeds, but it is not. Morality has very little to do with psychology.

It may, however, be wise to recall that when we critically evaluate the few explanations to which all analysis seems to lead, we discover something that was already noticeable in Freud's *Interpretation of Dreams*: the extreme intensity and the astonishing prevalence of jealousy, envy or greed. Our greedy Mrs. A. is thus a characteristic representative of mankind as revealed in analysis. Pastry is at issue seldom, but power almost always; the refusal to relinquish anything one covets for oneself, whether it be mother, father, or someone or something else constitutes an assertion of power. Competition rules supreme. Motives for behavior and guilt feelings are everywhere the same. Everywhere it is a question of moral dogs-in-the-manger.

We can consider consciousness in an entirely different context, and perhaps by so doing we may arrive at a fuller understanding of this strange phenomenon. The raw material of consciousness is not primarily the relationship of the aware individual to himself and others, but his relationship to *time*, the time he lives in. We only exist in time insofar as it intrudes upon us, unfolds with us, and then rolls up around us. Time articulates our conscious being. We are in it like a swimmer who can never leave the water and for that reason will drown in it some day. That is, we consume time and it consumes us, until finally it swallows us up.

Consciousness, in this view, is essentially a conscious existing in time. It lends the fleeting moment excessive significance and simultaneously diminishes it by banishing into the past all those vanished moments which were once just as precious. And we incorporate the present moment into a system of comparison and classification which is based on and determined by the past.

Alfred Adler contended that this view is only partially accurate and by no means decisive. The individual, he felt, is either "prospective" or he is psychically nonexistent: that is one of the central tenets of individual psychology. The present moment *does* fit in with all that has gone before, but we experience, grasp and interpret it, try to hold it back or rush past it because we are unconditionally pledged to the future. In actual fact we judge the present according to a system which is shaped by our conscious or subconscious prospect for life.

This is the concept of causal finality, which Adler believed both inherent in the human condition and essential to understanding that condition. Adler was not the only man to insist that a human being without finality can neither be conceived nor understood. But can one understand what finality entails without knowing where it originates? At some time, Adler felt, an individual forms a suggestive image of future happiness; the search for this happiness then becomes an unalterable *life plan*. The ideal image does not appear out of the blue; it grows out of particular, usually incompletely understood experiences. Before launching into a lengthy and complicated discussion of the types of experience involved, one might be tempted to say that they all add up to the same thing, namely causality. The experiences which lead to the establishment of goals and, according to the finalists, determine personality development all function within a causal system.

Upon closer scrutiny, Adler's finalism turns out to be less finalism than determinism riddled with holes. Adler was but one of many to embrace this seemingly contradictory concept. Karl Marx of course comes to mind: the founder of "scientific socialism" spent almost a lifetime constructing arguments to prove that the replacement of antagonistic capitalist class society by classless socialism was clearly determined and in fact imminent. But that did not prevent him from declaring, apparently in contradiction of himself and his works (but perhaps in some strange dialectical harmony with them) that capitalist society would have to be destroyed, either by socialism or, on the contrary, by barbarism. This deterministic prophecy reminds me of the well-trained dachshund in the old Austrian joke who, in response to his master's imperious question, "Are you coming—or not?" comes—or does not. The psychologist must ascertain whether certain events in early childhood absolutely determine the character of the individual. Long before Freud, there prevailed a dramatic concept of life according to which unusual and above all traumatic experiences were responsible for individual development. The term "psychic trauma" may be used to describe those psychically damaging experiences which jolt the child's already precarious equilibrium so violently that it can never be restored without special assistance. Adler never denied that something similar happens to every child. But even when he still played a leading role in psychoanalytic circles, he had become convinced that no event, no experience and none of their direct consequences could in themselves determine anything. Adler noted that important events often go unnoticed or that their effects quickly evaporate because they are somehow not pertinent, while events which are objectively much less important can have such an impact that their effects continue to turn up for years, decades or a lifetime in involuntary associations, in dreams and of course in childhood memories.

Let us try an experiment. Try to think spontaneously of three childhood experiences. Plan to recall those of earliest childhood, but do not reject any memories that surface, even if they clearly belong to a later period. Most people usually find to their amazement that these recollections center around insignificant episodes which have in fact had no repercussions. Furthermore, the attitude toward life revealed in or deducible from these recollections will match their present attitude.

It is also noteworthy that the three or four recollections, if accurately interpreted, form a logical progression like the acts of a play. The full import emerges only from the totality, or from the last scene. For Alfred Adler's concept of character formation it is thus less important what a child actually experiences than how he comprehends and evaluates it. Another example, from the annals of Marxism, may help clarify this point.

From 1929 onward, the Great Depression shook the entire capitalist world to its very foundations, but especially highly industrialized Germany with its enormous proletariat. In the Marxist sense the Depression produced the necessary preconditions for the immediate creation of a revolutionary situation, from which the working class would quickly emerge victorious. But as we know, the willingness of the workers to intensify the class struggle by means of ever longer and bigger strikes and their readiness to fight to the last man diminished markedly during those years. Fear of growing unemployment did not have the expected effect of bolstering their revolutionary élan; it lamed their morale. The victory of fascist movements in Germany and elsewhere and the stability of the existing regimes in the West proved that the absolute pauperization of millions of farmers and workers, prophesied by Marx and spawned by the Depression, did not necessarily encourage the forces of revolution; under certain conditions it could result in counter-revolution and even traditional reaction.

One could of course reply that everything depended on the degree of class consciousness among workingmen, on their political maturity. But if a crisis of such cosmic dimensions and such unprecedented severity does not promote the consciousness-raising process—and this in a country which has for decades made exceptionally well-organized efforts in this direction—then what *does* this evolution, this revolutionary thrust of the working class and its historical awareness depend on? The alternative of socialism or barbarism formulated by Marx, but never really taken seriously, proved temporarily to be quite accurate. In the country of the proletarian revolution of 1917, socialism soon soured and turned into a permanent totalitarian counter-revolution; in Germany the Nazis won out, barbarism triumphed. Everywhere the vanquished bowed their heads in submission.

One can see that even in macro- or social psychology a flawless picture of determinism is difficult to compose. Freud's causal concept of trauma, on the other hand, is based on a rigidly deterministic theory of psychic life. He sees psychic life as the normal or disturbed functioning of various mechanisms. Adler's conception is considerably less scientific, for he attributes great importance to an element of irrationality. This he does without inclining to the mystical or being attracted by the irrational per se. It is not his interpretations which are irrational but their subject matter—man, especially in his origins. Adler commented:

We orient ourselves according to a fixed point which we have artificially created, which does not in reality exist, a fiction. This assumption is necessary because of the inadequacy of our psychic life. It is very similar to other fictions which are used in other sciences, such as the division of the earth by non-existent, but highly useful meridians. In the case of all psychic fictions we have to do with the following: we assume a fixed point even though closer observation forces us to admit that it does not exist. The purpose of this assumption is simply to orient ourselves in the chaos of existence, so that we can arrive at some apperception of relative values. The advantage is that we can categorize every sensation and every sentiment according to this fixed point, once we have assumed it.

Individual Psychology, therefore, creates for itself a heuristic system and method: to regard human behavior and understand it as though a final constellation of relationships were produced under the influence of the striving for a definite goal upon the basic inherited potentialities of the organism. Our experience, however, has shown us that the assumption of a striving for a goal is more than simply a convenient fiction. It has shown itself to be largely coincident with the actual facts in its fundamentals, whether these facts are to be found in the conscious or unconscious life.[2]

Experience suggests the unfortunately mundane observation that we are obliged to develop consciousness at the age clearly most unsuited to the task. It would of course be much more rational for us to face this task after our faculties had been fully developed, in our mature years. But the child cannot escape the chore, and under this constant pressure invents a stratagem for coping with it, the procedure of "as if-ing," whose advantages were impressively demonstrated by the philosopher Hans Vaihinger.[3] Of this fiction Adler rightly said that it is useful both for

the child's acquisition of consciousness and for psychological study of that process.

We say "acquisition of consciousness." But such an expression is not very precise and not always appropriate.
Consciousness is not merely a reflection of reality, but a
much more complex affair. Here the process of becoming
constitutes an act; *becoming* conscious entails *making* conscious. The phenomenon is partly one of receptivity, especially with regard to the stimuli transmitted to us by our
senses, but much more significant is the active process that
first creates and then gradually and selectively establishes
awareness.

Our consciousness stores actualized, filled-in time. Thus
we obtain a continuity without which we would have to
begin our self-development anew each day of our life. The
human being would have perished like many animals similar to him had he not succeeded in becoming such a
historical entity. Man has survived only because he is able
to accumulate time and keep his own experience and that
of others on tap, preserving the past within the present.

We are speaking here of the highest degree of consciousness, the consciousness of consciousness. To Socrates
the important thing was knowledge of knowledge. The
individual who remembers something knows that he is
who he is, and also he whom he remembers—that is, he
whom he was and no longer is. So consciousness of consciousness would be the confrontation of two degrees of
knowledge, two certainties and two different participants
in the same experience. From the vantage point of this
super-consciousness Rousseau could undertake to write
his *Confessions*, to "portray his spiritual state in two
guises," i.e., as he had felt it at the moment of the experi-

ences themselves and as he perceived it much later when
he was describing them. From a similar vantage point Mar-
cel Proust set out in search of "things past."

How complex this system of self-referral is can also be
seen in the fact that we feel ourselves to be old by comparison with our childhood and youth, and yet we also
experience each day as a new first day, on which everything could begin from scratch. We can see time from
both ends because we simultaneously move along through
time and are borne along by it. Though we are always the
children we once were, we also perceive more clearly than
any outside observer that we are filling ourselves up more
and more with a time that is different from that of our
youth, with a time that will destroy us from within. By
moving away from our beginnings we initiate an unconscious process of dis-identification which can in time produce terrifying results. Experiences preserved in all their
immediacy by consciousness become autonomous and degenerate into recollections: we do still know that it *was*
us, but once this process takes place we are aware that it
no longer *is* us.

Adler's position on the question of consciousness and
the unconscious was that consciousness develops in compensation for the biological inferiority of the child. Without this compensation the unceasing goal-directed motion
that is psychic life would not develop; it would be out of
the question because there would be no preservation of
time.

Consciousness appears in various degrees of clarity and
intensity. It maintains a constantly up-dated résumé of
what the individual has understood of the world, of himself, of his relations to others and theirs to him. It is a

reservoir of confusion, misunderstandings, misconceptions. Aspects of life which have not been fully grasped may lack clear outlines by comparison with secure knowledge, yet under some circumstances, aspects of our lives that we have not fully understood can have much more influence on how we see the world than can well-understood experiences. Such uncomprehended material neither undergoes nor causes repression; in the first phase of consciousness-formation it is merely a product of our inability not to go astray here and there. During this first phase we develop the tendency to regard things which only merit "as if" status as proven, hard facts. Thus imperfect understanding is natural and common, the more so since it is often not recognized for what it is.

In a second phase consciousness no longer functions as a storehouse for time past; it becomes as a filter. Here goal-setting, also launched on the basis of "as if" assumptions, takes on decisive importance. The goal determines the principle of choice according to which the child very early learns to distinguish between the helpful and the harmful. Consciousness becomes a tool in a polarization process. Anything perceived as harmful, negative, undesirable or unpleasant need not even be repressed, for we see it already distorted, and we can immediately either ignore it or else press it into the services of a goal. This process can take very different forms. One of them, although neither the most common nor the most effective, is repression. The good soldier Schweik protects himself from the consequences of his actions by pointing out that he is an officially certified idiot. We all ward off uncomfortable realizations by means of a "private logic," as Adler called it, custom-made ignorance or stubborn indifference. We happen to look the other way or manage to be occupied with something else and have no time for anything which does not suit our purposes. No one is so deaf as he who will not hear.

But where does this principle of selective inattention come from? According to Adler, one must take a person's entire individual constellation into account when looking for the answer to this question. One should note especially the individual's degree of self-esteem and the courage which manifests itself in his deeds—not in his self-image. An adequate, stable sense of his own worth and proven psychic courage allows an individual to open himself boldly to the world. Almost every truth suits his purposes, for there is no insight, no facet of knowledge which he must block out for fear of its sowing doubt and insecurity in him. The way he approaches reality is open-ended. He can take an intense interest in matters which are unfamiliar to him. In other words, he faces life with that readiness for active participation which is engendered by social interest. Courage, social interest, consciousness as self-awareness, as social awareness and as a durable form of participation in the life of the community—all this, according to Adler, forms an indissoluble unity.

I shall return again and again to the problems of consciousness, unconsciousness and the uncomprehended in our experience. What I have said about these matters in this chapter is intended to serve as preparation for what follows. But it is not too early to warn the reader that nothing I have said so far about consciousness and nothing I shall say in the pages to come really solves the problem or formulates it in any definitive manner. The most we can hope for is an approximation.

Chapter IV

A DLER IS FAMOUS all over the world for the term "inferiority complex," which he coined—though there are many misinformed or biased contemporaries who would attribute this concept to Freud. As the French say, *"On ne prête qu'aux riches."*

It was Carl G. Jung who introduced the concept of the complex to modern psychology, and since then it has become the most often used and most frequently misused catchword. Jung defined the complex as

psychic contents which are outside the control of the conscious mind. They have been split off from consciousness and lead a separate existence in the unconscious, being at all times ready to hinder or to reinforce the conscious intentions.[1]

Elsewhere he remarked that the complex is a psychic force which sometimes puts individual freedom temporarily out of commission.

Adler's theory of inferiority feelings, which he originally conceived in connection with his research in the field of congenital organ inferiorities, has firm foundations, even without having any connection whatsoever with the complex theory. The expression "inferiority *complex*," which he used here and there only in later years, coincides only partially with the Jungian definition.

The inferiority feeling has assumed overwhelming importance in the field of comparative individual psychology because every human being feels himself directly spoken to by this expression. Even if he rejects the idea as something unpleasant, he cannot escape the suspicion that it does pertain to him, that it affects and unmasks him. In a dialogue-psychology like Adler's, which sees every individual more as a *you* than as a *he* or a *she*, it is important that the individual in question feel implicated in the good or the bad sense, that he recognize himself. Whether the feeling of inferiority springs from accurate or inaccurate perceptions or comparisons, it aims for its own disappearance; it is fundamentally incompatible with the self-awareness of the individual, with his needs and his objectives.

There is no peculiarity, no situation, no event, no action, no experience which cannot produce feelings of inferiority. Such feelings appear at every age, but most frequently during the years of development; they attack a person because he feels too tall or too short; because he feels interchangeable with everyone else or far too different; because his head is too long or too round; because his hair is blond or black or red; because he has too small or too narrow a nose; because he thinks he has noticeably handsome or ugly parents who are either too haughty or too self-effacing; because he is the oldest or the youngest child or the child in the middle; because he has a brown patch on his hand or a wart on his ear. He can experience feelings of inferiority because a schoolmate or a neighbor has greater success, because only he has been praised, because the cherries bloom earlier in his garden or because his gladioli are redder. . . . He can be tormented by these feelings because he feels he has received insufficient attention or, on the other hand, too much; because advantages which he does not have are constantly hailed and because defects for which he was once reproved are criticized. . . . The list could go on forever. The important thing for Adler was this: the actual existence of inferiority caused by a physical shortcoming, or, as Adler termed it, an inferior organ, by frequent illness, by an unfavorable place in the birth-order, by the social, economic, religious or national situation of the family, conditions the creation and the degree of inferiority feelings but does not determine them. Often a child remains oblivious to his actual disadvantages and handicaps. He may not see his own small stature as a drawback, for example. On the other hand, one encounters many examples of inferiority feelings for which no objective basis exists. Almost everyone can remember such strange sensitivities from his childhood and the suffering they occasioned him. And then one day it turned out that the whole thing had grown out of an error, a misunderstanding of something an adult had said or a silly joke one should not have taken seriously.

The fact remains that inferiority feelings are never without basis but are very seldom really justified. They exert a disheartening influence, but they also have the dialectical effect of producing positive compensation. They assume an unusual importance in the unending process of our self-education. They heighten our sensitivity, which along with certain disadvantages has the positive effect of refining our receptivity and sharpening our perceptions. The sensitive individual is more subject to the real and imagined difficulties of life than the less sensitive one. At the same time he develops his feel for nuances, for fine shades, for tonalities. This is true even of the neurotic; a jealous person might harbor destructive suspicions, but in order to nourish these he must amass perceptions of incredible precision. The same is true of certain illnesses, which considerably heighten the keenness of our senses and our aesthetic sensibility. The same sensitivity which makes for unbearable feelings of inferiority helps create that psychic superperformance that Adler called compensation.

In his *Study of Organ Inferiority* Adler pointed out that an inferior organ can only achieve normal function with the help of increased brain performance. One can all the better understand that in his research on inferiority feelings Adler was always anxious to discover to what degree they had an objective basis and what specifically that basis was. But for him the most pressing problem was that of compensatory performance: how does the affected individual react to the discovery of insufficiency in himself? What does he do with his sense of inferiority? What heights of performance does he achieve in order to make up for it? This concern was the source of Adler's skeptical attitude toward the notion of psychic heredity; he considered that what a person inherits is less important than what he makes of it. This same attitude can be found in almost all educators and almost all schools of interpretive psychology.

But if we are to believe that everything depends on how a person copes with his inferiority feelings and that his character is decisively influenced by these feelings and the manner in which he compensates for them, we seemingly find ourselves going in circles. Does an individual actually decide to compensate, to overcompensate or to capitulate and seek refuge in weakness? Is it a matter of choice, and if so, when is the choice made? While the personality is still developing, that much is clear, but how and on what basis?

Long before Jean-Paul Sartre (who unconsciously is a perfect Adlerian in many respects), long before many other thinkers of the last few decades, Alfred Adler recognized the question of choice as the central problem in character formation. His discovery of the "as if" mechanism finally persuaded him that human development and character formation involve something that one must recognize as creative will or a creative force. In the last analysis we cannot really prophesy anything but the past. When we know how things have turned out and have traced the developmental process, we are able to say quite modestly, "This is how it occurred, therefore it had to occur this way; it could not have happened any other way." But we cannot foresee anything as inevitable.

One of the points of disagreement which was to come between Adler and me had to do precisely with this idea, which I at the time rejected as idealistic and therefore suspect, indeed reactionary. Though I must now confess that my aversion to this conception has diminished considerably, I still do not believe that Adler was completely right. So today all that separates me from Adler on this subject is my inclination to make do without an adequate explanation. It is a negative, perhaps sad position, but it protects me from drawing hasty conclusions and gives me the courage to accept my lack of knowledge and understanding.

Be that as it may, it is safe to say that the individual usually chooses his course in ignorance, with little comprehension and even less experience, a course he will follow for the rest of his life. The first stage of character formation reached by this path, often by way of a difficult detour, is that of compensation, a style of action and of overcoming disabilities that will characterize the person from then on.

Some authors critical of the principles of individual psychology, accuse Adler of denying the force of human drives. They claim he regarded the will-to-power as the sole motivation for all human acts and behavior. Adler's analyst critics contend that he wanted to explain all human relations, including sexuality, as well as societal, occupational and philosophical problems by the drive for power. As I suggested earlier, there was a relatively short phase in the development of individual psychology during which Adler tended to attribute the predominant role in emotional life to the will-to-power. It is difficult to determine whether or not the influence of Nietzsche, which was beginning to make itself felt in the early twentieth century, prompted Adler to overestimate the will-to-power. Adler's character and his keen appreciation of the human comedy suggest that he would himself have arrived at the same insights which the philosopher so brilliantly formulated. Adler's path would in any case have led to analytic psychology. There is no doubt that Nietzsche thought of the will-to-power as the trait of a nobler form of man, as the means and end of overcoming humanness in favor of the superman, as a sublime quality, a new, supreme form of virtue.

Nothing could be more contrary to this idea than Adler's concept of the *drive for power*. For him any drive for power is the inefficient attempt of a deeply discouraged, tormented individual to overcompensate for his feelings of inferiority. Such an individual despairs of gaining a sense of his own worth under normal circumstances—that is, the circumstances that suffice for others. His oppressive feelings can be counteracted in his imagination and in his more or less unconscious choice of an ideal by an image of infinite superiority and unlimited power: a likeness to God. Thus for individual psychology the will-to-power certainly does not express unassailable superiority or a sovereign sense of security or even superhumanness; on the contrary, it is compelling proof of the extreme insecurity of the person who thirsts for power and of his inability to engage in normal social intercourse, his failure in all human relations.

It is clear, then, that the drive for power in Adler's sense has nothing in common with Nietzsche's will-to-power. The question remains: Why did Adler judge this to be such an important phenomenon, as important as Freud's Oedipus complex? and is partially answered in the following passage:

The tendency to push into the limelight, to compel the attention of parents, makes itself felt in the first days of life. Here are found the first indications of the awakening desire for recognition developing itself under the concomitant influence of the sense of inferiority, with its purpose the attainment of a goal in which the individual is seemingly superior to his environment. . . . His goal is so constructed that its achievement promises the possibility either of a sentiment of superiority, or an evaluation of the personality to such a degree that life seems worth living. It is this goal which gives value to our sensations, which links and co-ordinates our sentiments, which shapes our imagination and directs our creative powers, determines what we shall remember and what we must forget. . . . When we question how we can most advantageously oppose the development of the striving for power, this most prominent evil of our civilization, we are faced with a difficulty, for this striving begins when the child cannot be easily approached. . . . But *living* with the child at this time does offer an opportunity to so develop his social feeling that the striving for personal power becomes a negligible factor.

A further difficulty lies in the fact that children do not express their striving for power openly, but hide it under the guise of charity and tenderness, and carry out their work behind a veil. Modestly, they expect to escape disclosure in this way. An uninhibited striving for power is capable of producing degenerations in the psychic development of the child, an exaggerated drive for security and might, may change courage to impudence, obedience into cowardice, tenderness into subtle treachery for dominating the world.[2]

These sentences are taken from *Understanding Human Nature*, Adler's most successful book. The work, published in 1927, was directed at a general audience, hence the nontechnical language. But it contains throughout formulations which reveal Adler's final position on most of the psychological problems that occupied him all his life. For this reason the reader who is familiar with *The Neurotic Constitution* and *The Practice and Theory of Individual Psychology* should read *Understanding Human Nature* very carefully. In spite of certain awkwardnesses of expression stemming from the fact that the work is essentially a collection of lectures delivered in Vienna and in foreign countries by the founder of individual psychology, this book offers many precise definitions and welcome distinctions and nuances. The reader must be warned, however, that here Adler used the expressions "desire for recognition," "desire for superiority," and "drive for power" interchangeably, because these tendencies are all occasioned by negative feelings, feelings of inadequacy, inferiority and instability. These three expressions are not identical in meaning, however, and we shall see how different, for instance, the desire for recognition is from the drive for power. Desire for recognition and desire for personal dominance obviously form part of the eternal human comedy, while the desire for power begins on its periphery and leads from there to tragedy: to repression, degradation and destruction of everything human. But let us linger for a moment with the comedy; much of what we shall discuss here and in the following chapters belongs to it. Comedy is based on a buildup of misunderstandings. Each misunderstanding may seem to correct the preceding one but in fact only succeeds in further complicating matters.

Goethe's pronouncement in *Faust*, "Man errs as long as he strives," [3] was intended seriously, but Aristophanes, Molière, Goldoni, Nestroy and the like could have used the same statement as a motto for their comedies. In Nietzsche's amoral analytical works, above all in *Human All Too Human, Beyond Good and Evil, The Genealogy of Morals* and many of his aphorisms, one finds countless descriptions and characterizations of human absurdity. Nietzsche laughs far less often than he scoffs. When I, an enthusiastic reader of Nietzsche, met Adler and began to grasp his view of man, I recognized that he was a spiritual descendant of Nietzsche the unmasking psychologist, but that he far surpassed his predecessor and, furthermore, was moving in an almost diametrically opposite direction.

Nietzsche sees man as simultaneously ridiculous and "a searing shame." Adler, also, sees the absurdity of man, a creature who is fundamentally harmless, but also danger-ous—particularly to himself.

Many ironists before and after Nietzsche have depicted the infinite absurdity of social life and conversation. Nietzsche describes a typical conversation in a brief passage entitled "A Comedy Scene that Occurs in Real Life":

A person thinks up a clever opinion on a certain topic and plans to produce it in company. Now the comedy would show how he spreads all his sails to reach the crucial point and to take the others on board where he can throw in his remark; how he continually tries to guide the conversation in that direction, occasionally loses his bearings, then veers back on course, and finally arrives at the critical moment: his breath almost fails him—and just then someone comes out with his very own observation. What will he do? Argue against his own opinion? [4]

It is rare conversation in which at least one of the participants is not more anxious to gain recognition for himself than to argue for what he considers to be the truth. For this reason conversation usually becomes shadowboxing, with the participants slyly pretending to engage in substantive argument in order to obtain confirmation from the others. One method is to stage melodramatic scenes: many classic comedies begin with a character arriving all breathless to deliver some sensational news. He knows something the others cannot even suspect. This he exploits until there is no one left whom he has not made aware of his superiority.

All of this is perfectly harmless, though ludicrous. But why do individuals want to call attention to themselves in such ways? Why do even small children use every imaginable ruse to become the focus of interest? Adler tells us: "It is the feeling of inferiority, inadequacy, insecurity, which determines the goal of an individual's existence." [5]

The motivation behind man's foolish behavior is by no means an occasion for mirth. What makes this exertion seem so funny is the sheer pointlessness of it. An example:

In a film we see Charlie Chaplin sleeping on a fenced-in

construction site, with only the sky as a roof. The sleeper suddenly becomes restless, starts up and looks around him, aware that he feels chilly. He discovers a small chink in the wooden fence, goes over and plugs it with a piece of newspaper, and then contentedly lies down again.

The disproportion between the effect of the cold evening air all around and the air seeping through the tiny hole produces the comic effect. We laugh at the lengths to which a human being will go for a trivial matter while ignoring matters of great importance. This incident also exemplifies another kind of inadequacy, one which Adler saw as the basis of all humor, but especially of Jewish humor: the conjunction between two separate frames of reference.

In the eternal human comedy the need for superiority and uncontested recognition may motivate either a harmless battle for appearances or the competitive struggle of life, which can take on dangerous dimensions even when it is not an actual struggle for existence. However, it is psychologically significant that the value of these exertions begins to diminish as soon as their goal is achieved. Actually the goal remains just as distant, for it moves in the same direction, and at the same speed, as he who pursues it.

Yet there is a biologically well-founded argument in favor of the attempt to attract attention. It is unquestionably of vital importance for the helpless child constantly to attract the interest of those around him in order not to be forgotten and neglected. Crying and screaming are in fact essential. But the child soon discovers that he can summon an adult in this manner even when he does not need help. Thus he invents a signal which he can use—and misuse—at his convenience. The child creates a sort of conditioned reflex in adults which he utilizes from time to time, often merely to combat boredom. The need to be noticed and to remain the center of attention can, under certain circumstances, be viewed as an outgrowth of the child's earliest experiences.

Let us consider the case of an older child, a schoolboy. He has difficulty keeping up with the class, perhaps because he started school a few weeks late and cannot quite catch up by himself, or because he spends the night in a small room with two younger children and his sleep is so often disturbed that he is tired the next morning. Or because he is near-sighted without knowing it and sits too far from the board. His seeming slowness provokes the teacher more and more often to unkind remarks, and he becomes the butt of the other children's scorn. He gives no indication of how much he suffers from all this, but one day after a scuffle, he discovers that he does not need the others—not the praise of the teacher, which only the others receive anyway, and not the friendship of his classmates, which is denied to him in any case. Thus he is, like Shakespeare's Richard III, "determined to prove a villain," that is, the rowdy of the class, to the extent his strength permits, but more especially the buffoon. In this role he strides from success to success. With one grimace he is able to bring the scoffers to his side. With a seemingly involuntary gross gesture, with challenging, improper or impudent responses—with every prank he seems to draw the attention of the class to himself, and he seems to be under the irresistible sway of this behavior. He is made to stand in the corner, or undergo other punishment. He has to stay after class, and every day he has to do new disciplinary exercises. Relentlessly his course moves downward, as he faces repeated disciplinary action, but the more he loses the more he seems to feel he has won. He is at once a problem child and a jester. He impresses the other children, whether they laugh at his pranks or at him, for he seems to be impervious to the authority for which they feel respect and awe. Conceivably this prankster could develop his particular form of overcompensation into a regular profession for later life.

The famous Yiddish writer Sholem Aleichem had a harsh stepmother who tyrannized and plagued him ceaselessly. The boy took revenge in his moments of despair by imitating the words and gestures of his tormentor. In addition he put together a small dictionary of the curses and invectives used by his stepmother.

The readers of his humorous stories have for many years wondered at the great precision with which he recreates the speech and gestures of his characters. Without meaning to explain away his unusual gifts or belittle his worldly wisdom, I might point out that his childhood, and the compensatory mischief-making in which he found comfort and consolation were excellent preparation for his future occupation and avocation. He made his listeners and readers laugh; most of them discovered only later, and to their great surprise, that the stories with which he had entertained them were almost without exception sad in content.

Anyone who has ever worked with a mischievous child, one who has become an outsider to his class, to his little society, must have been impressed by the great sadness that seemed to lurk just below the surface of his constant merriment. It was not immaterial to such a child that he was the worst pupil in the school and that at home he was always showered with abuse and reproaches because of it. I was deeply affected when in the case of one such child—he was a fatherless boy of seven—I began to think that no other fate was possible, no matter what he did. Just a few months of desolation will suffice to reduce a human being to such a state of self-alienation that he ends by experiencing his own deeds as hostile acts.

In connection with such cases a question arises: If the conscious mind accepts, processes and actualizes only that which suits a person's purposes, why does it permit feelings of inferiority, which are unpleasant, even tormenting, and certainly unwelcome to everyone? A similar question arises in connection with the psychoanalytical theory on the power of wishes in dreams; for there are so many distressing, frightening dreams and nightmares, and the dreamer remembers them all the more clearly because they wrench him violently out of his sleep.

The feeling of inferiority is intolerable; it weakens or utterly consumes other emotions. Inferiority feelings create a compulsion to compare, using a mainly negative measuring stick; attributes which one does not possess are often greatly overvalued, precisely because one finds them in others and not in oneself. This compulsion to compare and to evaluate upsets a person's equilibrium when feelings of inferiority and insecurity turn into complexes. Then a vicious circle is set in motion: the transformed feelings of inferiority become not only acceptable but necessary, so that escapism may be interpreted as a triumph. What we have here is not merely a quantitatively increased feeling of inferiority but also its false, i.e., fictitious, compensation. The problem is actually not overcome; it is merely concealed—and, in fact, aggravated.

The young girl who refuses to go dancing on the grounds that because of her ugly legs no one will ask her to dance, now makes her inferiority complex into a source of security. She begins by downgrading girls who do go dancing, saying that one lowers oneself when one waits to

be asked to dance. Before her complex provides her with
an escape, she occasionally succumbs to the temptation and
allows herself to be talked into going to a ball. But she
quickly withdraws, explaining to her girl friends (even be-
lieving it herself) that she cannot stand the clammy hands
of her partners and the smell of bodies in the dance hall, not
that she is running away because she is afraid of not being
asked to dance. And finally the dramatic highlight: she
suffers a fainting fit, which is all the more alarming since
no one seems to notice it at first; all her girl friends are on
the dance floor. From this point on the feeling of inferiority will seem less concrete; she will no longer blame her
reticence on this or that aesthetic objection, but will base
it on the impressive argument that of course she cannot
risk another fainting attack—even if all the partners in the
world are waiting for her.

Here the inferiority complex is speaking; it uses the imperative "organ dialect," Adler's term for the neurotically
determined misuse of an organ, usually an inferior one.
According to Jung's definition we are dealing here with
psychic contents which lead a life of their own and can
either interfere with or facilitate conscious actions. But
Jung also says that these contents become divorced from
consciousness. Here this is not the case, for here we have a
game of self-deception carried out in semidarkness; the
process is by no means fully unconscious. A monologue is
masked as a dialogue between an innocent, obedient psyche
and an inconsiderate, disruptive body. The fear of fainting provides justification, even a necessity, for the girl to
avoid not only dancing partners but all society, thus allowing her to conceal the problem behind a pseudonym. It is
true that she has seizures, so she is not lying, but she is lying
with the truth. Adler, who liked to use military metaphors,

spoke of the retreat to a "secondary theater of war," where victory is all the more certain because one does not encounter the enemy and can triumph without actual combat.

Often, men and women of slight physical attractions develop a capacity for forceful self-advertisement, and as specialists in the daily comedy of erotic vanities they achieve considerable success. They become sexual headhunters. Women especially find it quite easy to modify their usual role by adroitly applying erotic aggressiveness. A woman easily conquers by letting the man think she is swept off her feet by his overpowering charm, drawn out of her usual reticence. Insistent courting by men and exaggerated flattery by women are some of the many forms of aggression that often compensate for feelings of inferiority.

In this case such feelings would suit the person's purposes. Whether or not a person's actions are compensatory in any given situation can be ascertained only by analyzing such behavior in connection with the individual's conduct of his whole life. Adler says that one must know the life style of a man if one is to know the man himself, that is, one must know the highways and byways, the shortcuts and detours by which the person plans to reach his chosen goal. The individual psychologist must perceive the tricks, stratagems and arrangements, or conversely the socially valuable compensations a person will utilize in seeking to come to terms with himself.

If amnesia suddenly cut a person off from his past, he would suffer a loss of identity for the duration of the disorder. But if a boundless despair or a deadly threat, for example, were to cut him off from the future, he would no longer be able to live. Nothing that we do or plan makes any sense if the aftermath, the subsequent moment, the coming day, is no longer implied.

For the human being who looks always ahead, the future is that-which-should-be, the realm of fulfilled desires, total unassailable freedom, mastery over life. Only reconciliation of that-which-is with that-which-should-be enables one to come to terms with oneself. But does that-which-should-be actually consist of superiority, recognition, even power? Is it really important always to be the center of attention, to be fondled, cared for, never punished, always praised and loved? And should that be the case merely because positions of inferiority and feelings of insecurity are unbearable, intolerable? Are there not more important things in life: religious feelings which reach beyond this world to link one with the cosmos; passions with which great ideas inspire us, exciting visions for the future of all mankind; love that transcends the passion to possess another and to hoard love and tenderness? Is man really only the ridiculous and infuriating hero of a comedy? Is he a stranger to real goodness, to genuine interest in the welfare of his brethren? Is he a stranger to the willingness to sacrifice himself for an ideal, for the community?

Alfred Adler gave a reassuring answer to all these questions: humanity's social interest, the saving force of communal feeling, was the basis of his optimistic view of the future of mankind. He was convinced that his teaching would gain more and more influence over educators, who would raise the new generation to become free, cooperative individuals filled with the sense of community. Wherever Adler found an attentive ear in the course of his world travels, he delivered this message. He continued to do so during the years when Hitler's and Stalin's rule over millions of people was growing ever more tyrannical and murderous. In the very years when World War II was being prepared, and concentration camps were springing up, still the skeptical, ironical observer and student of human nature continued to trust in the power of human community. He died two years before the outbreak of World War II, and so was spared witnessing the age of genocide.

Chapter V

THE FIRST PHASE of human life is of necessity parasitic, for infants and young children must be taken care of. As they are incapable of expressing their wishes clearly, adults must learn to interpret their needs and desires. During their earliest years children are receivers surrounded by givers, a situation that creates psychologically unfavorable factors for the initiation into life, significantly reinforcing the effects of organic difficulties that are present from the outset. To the parents, the child for whom they must provide everything is much more than a tiny living being who does nothing but demand and receive; his existence may be the greatest gift they will ever be given. The child for his part soon discovers that his very existence represents a magnificent accomplishment to those around him; and for decades, perhaps for his entire life, he will behave as if all he needed to contribute were his presence.

The child sometimes tries to keep his parents on a tight rein, using an impressive array of stratagems to force them to coddle him, but pampering usually diminishes when it ceases to be objectively necessary. Does that mean that we want to be loved and expect endless proofs of affection?

Certainly, but this says nothing unequivocal about reality. The love which a parasitic being expects should be called something else; likewise the love of the giver should be viewed somewhat critically. Parental doting, which expresses itself in endless indulgence and worship of the child, in letting him become a lazy tyrant, represents real love as little as jealousy does. It is only an indirect form of extreme self-indulgence, proof of parental incompetence and probably also of resistance to seeing the child become less dependent. The object of parental infatuation is supposed to remain an object, becoming independent as late as possible, preferably never. One is reminded of the rich masochist who bribes a poor man to beat and torture him. Only the humorless admirers of the Marquis de Sade will fail to recognize that the torturer becomes degraded to an object, to a misused stick, while the victim enjoys proof of his triumph with every blow he receives.

One of the most difficult tasks facing psychology is to illuminate the nature of human relationships and to interpret properly their intensity and the claims, expectations and functions that characterize them. The relations among parents, children and siblings may seem simple and "natural," but the same external forms can mean very different things. To let us move from the case of doting to the situation Freud considered paradigmatic, that of the incestuous love of the child for the mother, the Oedipus complex: analytical or "unmasking" psychologists, who are not intimidated by time-honored taboos, have often established that libidinous and nonlibidinous general ties between parents and children are no less frequent and much longer lasting and more significant than the specific relations between son and mother. One might speak of a reverse Oedipus complex. Parents who have lost all hope in their marriages, or parents who see old age as a threat to their enjoyment of life intrude with all the wiles of unhappy lovers or with insistent offers of help into the lives of their children. They try to assure themselves of a stable present by appealing to a distant past in which they were the givers who were loved boundlessly by the receivers. Apart from this reverse complex, I believe that Phaedra's love for Hippolytus is in every way more meaningful for the psychology of love than the relationship of Jocasta to Oedipus, regardless of whether Jocasta sees in Oedipus the ambitious young man and victorious protector or secretly suspects the cast-out son.

But let us return to the idea that the pampered child does not receive love, only the advantages and pleasures of a parasitic existence. Who would not question that this could be a dangerous, misleading first experience? However, normally it is quickly corrected when the child's circle widens; brothers and sisters and other children help the child find a new existence in which he gradually ceases to be an object of idolatry and becomes a subject among his peers. Here the child receives his first opportunity to develop his social interest, which Adler thought was inborn. The child may reject this opportunity, he may reject the community and fall back on the strength of weakness, on sickness and the refusal to communicate in an effort to retain his privileges. Here the child must make his first real decision.

Probably no one between the ages of three and five would freely renounce being coddled. The feeling of not being able to manage without constant tenderness is sometimes so strong that the child behaves as if he had been totally abandoned, as if on a warm summer day winter had suddenly set in. When one studies the childhood of neurotics, one often encounters what might be called a "psychic cold": it is caused by an actual or imagined change in the emotional temperature, for example, the birth of a brother or sister.

The despotically passive, self-assertive, pampered child can succeed only at the expense of others. The active child who washes and dresses himself, ties his own shoes, and wants to open doors, is seen by contrast to have entered the first phase of a process which leads to awareness of his environment, that is, consciousness of the fact that for everyone else he is part of external reality, not solely an *I*. This awareness of external reality is the precondition for social interest, for in terms of real community all human beings are alike in that each has the right to be recognized both as an *I* and as external reality, and each shares a responsibility to recognize others in the same fashion. Each person also shares an obstacle, which probably no one can fully overcome: he is in constant contact only with himself and represents an uninterrupted continuity to himself. For oneself one is always home. . . .

In this sense we are all condemned to a certain egocentricity; we block our own path to community. The fairly common refusal of a child to talk, even after he has clearly grasped the meaning of many words, is an indication that he does not want to abandon his parasitic situation, for language is the first important means of socialization. The child demands that one speak to him, but he refuses to reciprocate. He can remain as good as dumb for months, sometimes years. To be sure, in most cases the child quickly gives up this resistance. Many factors play a part, not the least of which is the desire to be able to do as much as other children. The child meets the threat of inferiority by compensating. But since speech is indispensable for self-awareness; it is the most convincing means of self-expression, even though during his period of defiance the child seems to reject and disavow anything that comes from others. Even for that purpose language can be useful and the child soon discovers what it will later practice, especially in the family: that one must come close before one can create distance, his period of defiance is usually short-lived. For like most man-made tools, language is a means of shortening distances, a means of connecting as well as separating.

He who tries to remain a receiver wants to be loved without loving in return. His clearest memories are of un-fulfilled demands and expectations, moments in which the love of those around him seemed to falter or threatened to fail. And since such moments must occur sooner or later, the *experience of betrayal* is unavoidable. We have all had it, but for an extremely pampered child it takes on a de-cisive meaning and may make the choice of a neurotic way of life inevitable.

The traces of the experience of betrayal only *seem* to vanish in later life. The mind carefully stores them away; usually it is an insignificant episode that will turn up again and again in recollections of childhood. Often such recol-lections go back to a person's fourth, fifth or sixth year. The family spends the summer vacation in a big resort hotel. Awakened by the noise of strangers next door, the child, only four or five years old, cries out for his mother and father, but nobody comes. He goes to look for them and finds their room empty: they are gone, perhaps they will never return, they have forgotten their child. The par-ents soon come back, calm the child and put him to bed. That this sort of episode appears so often in childhood re-collections leads one to suspect that its meaning extends far beyond the experience of being unpleasantly awakened or the shock of finding oneself alone.

In fact, the experience has awakened a heretofore unknown mistrust: something in the behavior of the others, above all of the parents, is no longer quite right. Things will never be as they used to be. It is remarkable that the child so quickly hits on the melodramatic suspicion of betrayal. One can thus assume that it is not an isolated event like the night in the hotel that causes the experience of betrayal. In this as in other cases it is the result of a situation that has existed for some time. Situations are decisive at this age, when more than at any other behavior patterns are formed. The vacation experience only dramatizes a suspicion which has cropped up earlier—that the parents no longer love the child as they once did, or they do not love him at all, and that they intend to give all their tenderness to someone else, perhaps the younger child. The bases for such suspicions are numerous. One of the most important is the behavior of the parents, which in fact does change gradually during the transition period between the child's infancy and his third to fifth year. During this same phase the child encounters a phenomenon with which he will have to cope for a good while: the imperious authority of the older generation, of the father and mother, the kindergarten teacher and similar figures.

If the adult at first appeared to the child as the unconditional giver, he now reveals himself as the ruler who is always right and never has to give reasons when he dispenses orders, prohibitions and punishments. Precisely when the child becomes capable of reciprocity, when he realizes that he, too, must give, the behavior of the adults change: they now want to teach the child that he has no rights and is inferior because he lacks the knowledge and the ability to decide what he should and should not do. The parents can make all the decisions because they know everything; they know best. And for that reason they have the right to make demands, while the child has only the duty to obey without contradiction.

The change acts like bad magic: the child had begun to discover what freedom is and that he himself could be free. Now he must suffer limitation, authoritarian suppression of this freedom. Behavior or action which forces others into inferior positions and portrays these positions as unalterable and natural is characterized by individual psychologists as authority. The effect of authority is to add to feelings of inferiority and inadequacy feelings of subjugation. That alone would be enough to prove the harmfulness of authoritarian attitudes.

The child usually reacts with protracted resistance. He tries to assert himself, sometimes, even, by resisting justified demands and wishes. In this phase the desire to gain mastery over the mother or the father expresses itself in word and gesture. Here the Freudian concept of the incestuous libidinous bond and the Oedipus complex seem to find some support. Adler believed that the concept is not nearly as important as it seems; even if there is evidence of a libidinous relationship, it does not really determine the essence of the total relationship and the concomitant conflict. The child wants to dominate his mother and to this end utilizes either tyrannical love in the form of subjugation or submissive, unconditional love. In both cases the main objective is to secure the obedience of the mother and often the desirable side effect of a victory over the father, who usually embodies oppressive authority, for he forbids more than he indulges, punishes more often than he caresses. In this phase the sex of the subjugated parent hardly matters, and love can often be proffered to first one parent and then the other. This happens very often when a new-born child takes all the mother's time, so that the father is available. If this exchange succeeds, the relationship to the father will be more important for the rest of the child's life; it may even be the most important.

Is repudiation of parental authority a general phenomenon? The fact that many children feel more protected the more this authority makes itself felt would seem to belie this idea. However, one should not conclude that children allow themselves to be dominated without putting up resistance. A child raised in an authoritarian environment suffers an oppressive feeling of security vis-à-vis the outside world and tends to regard it as hostile territory. This creates in him the desire to see his parents impregnably strong and awe-inspiring to outsiders. At the same time, within the family he resists anything which would weaken his will or oppose his wishes. One often encounters this contradiction between domestic interests and foreign policy, so to speak, most frequently in marriages in which both partners have an equal interest in the success and prestige of the husband. Within the family the wife might constantly deprecate the qualities which she praises in her husband before others; these qualities frustrate her own efforts to feel superior, and thus she resents them.

Relationships among human beings are always part of an extremely complicated game, sometimes a war game with constantly shifting alliances. One can say that every human being seeks, creates, maintains or destroys his relationships according to a personal system of reference of which he is never wholly conscious. It is necessary to penetrate this system in order to predict with some certainty how a person will behave in different types of personal confrontation.

Adler considered that the place a child occupied in the family birth order was extremely important. For instance, he wrote about the second child:

The striving for power in the case of the second born also has its especial nuance. Second-born children are constantly under steam, striving for superiority under pressure: the race-course attitude which determines their activity in life is very evident in their actions. The fact that there is someone ahead of him who has already gained power is a strong stimulus for the second born. If he is enabled to develop his powers and takes up the battle with the first born he will usually move forward with a good deal of élan, the while the first born, possessing power, feels himself relatively secure until the second threatens to surpass him.[1]

Naturally the birth order must not be defined according to the official records but according to the actual situation. My own case might serve here as an example: although born the third son, I am in a sense the second-born, because the second son died early. Adler's characterization of the child in the sandwich position should apply to me, but that is not the case. In fact, I remained the youngest child in the family for five and one-half years. Not all that Adler has to say about the youngest is flattering:

No child likes to be the smallest, the one in whom no one has any confidence, all the time. Such knowledge stimulates a child to prove that he can do everything. His striving for power becomes markedly accentuated and we find the youngest very usually a man who has developed a desire to overcome all others, satisfied only with the very best.[2]

The significance of a child's place in the family cannot be denied, but in each case it must be examined like a piece in a puzzle, i.e., only in connection with all the other factors that determine character formation. One of these factors is sex. It makes a considerable difference whether one comes into the world as a male or a female child, particularly in families where boys are preferred to girls and where it is seen as a source of prestige that the first-born be male. There used to be many cases of women who were forced during childhood by tyrannical fathers to dress and behave as if they were boys. There were also cases, although not many, in which boys were forced to play the role of girls. In a male-dominated culture fear of the opposite sex in varying degrees is universal. Rejection of the woman's role by female children and the fear of males that they are insufficiently masculine and therefore inferior and inadequate crops up often, and not only in cases of neurosis. For this phenomenon Adler originated the term "masculine protest," applied primarily to women who reject their femaleness in their relation to the world around them and later to their marriages, constantly protesting against the injustice nature has wrought upon them.

Next to sex and birth order, one must of course consider the internal family situation, the successful or unsuccessful marriage of the parents, their life style, also the family's economic position and social status, and finally any membership in a religious, ethnic or political minority. In addition to the usual immense difficulties connected with obtaining psychological insight, there is the fundamental fact that the number of elements and factors which influence the development and actions of every person is practically endless. Thus we must find those elements that actually determine or help determine personal evolution. The psychologist must reconcile himself once and for all to the fact that he will never be able to account for all the factors, and that he can omit most of them—those that condition but do not determine the outcome. Sometimes he makes grave mistakes.

A love relationship at its height should be the most unproblematical relationship two people can enter into. The lovers live only for each other and feel happy only when they are together. Two Sunday's children joined forever, each forgetting himself for the sake of the other—could any other harmony be so well founded, so lasting? Yet in actuality arguments, conflicts, squabbles, confrontations, painful insults and frenetic hostilities occur much more frequently than in relationships that remain superficial, allowing room for soothing indifference and calm coexistence. How can it be that lovers who long for harmony and enjoy it thoroughly when they achieve it, can also so easily destroy that harmony for hours or even days on end, so that they fear it will never return? And how can one explain the hostility which without warning suddenly shoots up like a jet of flame and threatens to burn or consume them both?

For centuries people have been writing treatises on love. I am not referring to the "technical" manuals which promise sure erotic pleasure, but to books intended to serve the cause of sexual enlightenment, something which is still necessary, even today. Man may be born to love, but he still has to learn how; the experience of others may be useful and help avoid needless, humiliating experiences.

One would have expected psychoanalysis to provide the ultimate enlightenment on love, since sexual life occupies such an important place within psychoanalytic theory. One may say that this expectation has not been fulfilled. Understanding of human relationships in general and of love relationships in particular has been little advanced by Freud's teachings; on the contrary, it has often been muddled by clichés. This is all the more astonishing since from the beginning psychoanalysis placed the libido in the foreground of its psychological and psychopathological investigations, starting with revelations of the sexual impulses in small children. At best psychoanalysis offers microscopic detail, gigantic enlargements of tiny details. If this is true —and I think it so only to a small degree—one should point out the misleading impression which such exaggeration can produce. It is imperative that one never lose sight of actual dimensions and relationships, especially in the science of man.

Here one could reduce the difference between Freud's and Adler's theories to a simple formula, perhaps too simple a formula. Freud teaches that traumatic childhood experiences combine with incestuous fixations that are counteracted by reality, and with the inborn Oedipus complex; this conglomerate is influenced by the repressions imposed by civilization, and it determines every person's sexual life and thereby all his other relationships. Adler teaches that any individual's relationships, including the love relationship, are determined by the individual's specific reference system. The form this reference system takes depends on particular positions and situations—inferiority, inadequacy, lasting insecurity, the degree of social interest, the person's methods of compensation or negative compensation and his personal courage, especially his courage to accept lack of perfection. This last factor acquires great importance in a love relationship or in marriage because in them the ability to share and to forget oneself, the courage to accept others as equals, to see an *I* in the *you* and a *you* in the *I* is constantly put to the test. To return to an earlier example, the near-sighted young man who holds the woman on the floor with his knee: an Adlerian would deduce from such behavior that the young man harbors an insecurity which threatens the relationship, making it unlikely that he is able to be a good spouse and live *with* a person rather than merely alongside that person.

The divergence of the two schools stems not only from the differences in their concepts of psychology. The suppression and actual disfranchisement of women in male-dominated society which had existed for millennia was for Adler a fundamental state of affairs, whose importance for the psychological study of human relations in general and of family and love life in particular had to be acknowledged by all.

In accordance with the principles of individual psychology, masculine protest should be diagnosed and interpreted within its context. Adler sought the origins of masculine protest in social conditions, especially in patriarchy, whose establishment he attributed to an evolution which he saw in Marxist terms. Widespread changes in social conditions and general life style have in the meantime considerably reduced the role of masculine protest. And it is certainly noteworthy that one of the freest generations the world has ever known, present-day youth, a generation characterized by an unusual degree of sexual uninhibitedness and lack of prejudice, displays a tendency (and not only in hairstyle and dress) to eradicate or at least to mask the differences between the sexes.

This change in attitude cannot be traced back to the influence of psychoanalysis and its fight against castration-anxiety or to any influence of individual psychology and its discovery of masculine protest. These radical changes

in life style and behavior, and especially in the relationships of the generations and the sexes to one another, are
clearly determined by socioeconomic factors. We will
return to this subject later.

Reduction of the fundamental problems of authority in
society and in the family to the rule of the jealous father,
of revolution to the desire to kill the father that supposedly
holds revolutionaries together, is absurd; trying to explain
difficult and complicated relationships that exist among
human beings by a sexual jargon is also absurd; it may seem
profound and daring to bourgeois bigots and hypocrites,
but it is misleading and as shallowly pretentious as attempts
to explain Hamlet's tragedy as his desire to sleep with his
mother. Here the most important metaphor in psychoanalysis comes to mind: the myth of Oedipus and the
jargon derived from it, a jargon that obscures far more
than it reveals. For example, one can easily see that the
story would have turned out very differently if Oedipus
had killed a gardener, a day-laborer or a slave. The young
murderer would never have considered marrying a poor
widow. The aging Jocasta offered a kingdom as a dowry.

It is worth mentioning that the hero who gave his name
to the most famous complex in psychoanalysis was the
only individual whom fate did not allow to have an Oedipus complex! That Jocasta carried him in her womb for
nine months has no importance in this case, for the new-
born child was cast out immediately by his parents and
grew up with strangers; toward them he might have developed this complex, since he considered them his father
and mother. From the psychological point of view, Jocasta
was as little his mother as Hecuba, Laius as little his
father as Freud, in a sense *less* than the man who a thousand
years later would become the father of psychoanalysis.

To return to our topic, let us recall that when a person outgrows childhood, the love relationship often becomes the most important thing in his life. Why? His erotic and sexual needs offer part of the explanation. But in addition this is the first freely chosen relationship he enters into. Apart from childhood friendships, which rarely last long, this is the first test of his relation system outside the family, and it is a test that makes cheating difficult if not impossible. Only during the introductory phase of a love relationship does play-acting work effectively, not during the later stages.

In many relationships cheating expresses itself as lying, trickery, deceit and above all as pretense; deception and self-deception are difficult to tell apart. This is true especially of trivial relationships, but hardly of love and marriage; there cheating will quickly be perceived even by an unintelligent partner.

Everything said thus far about the individual and his development suggests that the relationship of a person to himself must be extremely problematical and complicated. But, once the personal system of reference has been established, this relationship gives all further relationships their distinctive character. The changes in an individual's relationship to himself provide the model for changes in his relations to others.

A person's ability to love depends on the relationship he has with himself. A person who is forever consoling, pampering, cajoling and watching over himself can hardly be expected to do the same for someone else. There is simply not enough concern left for another person: not enough attention, not enough intensity, and almost no energy; it's all expended on his own needs. One astonishing consequence of extreme self-centeredness is that the person cannot even love himself. He goes to great lengths to escape from himself, for he no longer wants to be identical with what he fears and rejects. He is incapable of loving himself as he is, and thus he falls in love with the person he pretends to be to others and to himself. This is the first form of cheating in human relations in which the deceiver and the deceived come together in one person; this is also the starting point for that human comedy we have mentioned so often. It is easy to understand that the biblical admonition to "love thy neighbor as thyself" often goes unheeded, for many people are not able to love themselves.

Consciousness can be many things, but since it always implies self-consciousness one cannot pass judgment on another person without implicating oneself—either through personal solidarity or antipathy. No matter whom an individual thinks about, he includes himself in the thought. This fact explains the amoralistic doubt toward the individual that underlies Adler's ironic interpretation of guilt feelings—self-blame—and the rationalizations that grow out of pangs of conscience. The psychologist of the individual quickly recognizes the hidden double of the dreamer: it is that character in a dream with whom the dreamer has the deepest sympathy, so that when something bad happens to him the dreamer starts out of his sleep in alarm. Everyone of us often needs coddling, as much as a small child does. We have all fallen out of warm nests; an eighty-year-old orphan might complain that the heartless world never offers him the aid to which a parentless child has a right.

Psychoanalysis sees the mother's womb as the lost Paradise; the event of being expelled from it, birth, is viewed by many psychoanalysts as the first and decisive trauma in the psychic life of every human being. Behavior characterized as regressive because it constitutes a return to childhood is interpreted as an attempt to find the way back to the refuge of the womb. One need not take the trauma of birth so seriously. One should simply bear in mind that our parasitic existence at the beginning of life in no way prepares us to change from receivers into givers. But we do manage this change, for when we reach the edge of the abyss the drive for self-preservation takes over: we want to live, and out of love for ourselves and our future we even believe that it is our duty to do so. In order to live we must learn to give.

Is individual psychology so pessimistic then that it does not see man as capable of overcoming egotism? No, on the contrary. Alfred Adler's optimism struck many of us as excessive at times; given the events of our century, we often found it hard to conceal our irritation.

Alfred Adler's great faith in man grew out of his conviction that human social failure was primarily due to man's not having learned to behave in a communal fashion. He firmly believed that one could *teach* virtue and methodically train people in communal feeling. In a word, Adler believed that one could promote socially useful behavior by convincing people that it best served their own interests.

Adler expected that social interest would single-handedly change the relation of the individual to himself and others in the direction of social utility and active solidarity. The same biological inferiority that he considered primarily responsible for the creation of inferiority feelings and efforts at compensation made participation in the community essential. Without social interest on the part of those around him, every child would be done for. Equally, every child had to learn to take his place in the human community, to recognize the essential compatibility between social interest and self-interest.

Adler often said, "When someone begins by saying, 'I fully intend . . . ,' he almost inevitably follows it up with the word 'but.' And only what he says after the 'but' should be taken seriously." A person who really wants to do something does not need to stress his good intentions. A student of human nature concentrates on what follows the "but" and judges what went before accordingly. We all know people who are constantly reproaching themselves, vastly exaggerating their own defects. By judging themselves this way they hope to prevent others from really judging them. Here, as with all forms of guilt that are not followed by corrective action, a saying of Martin Luther's is apropos: "Do not look at his mouth, look at his fist." One measures a person's social interest by what he does; then one can draw conclusions as to the value of his asseverations of good will. Adler's optimism applied not so much to what a person is but to what he could become, what he might be.

A man who had long suffered from severe depression sought out Adler and assured him that he would do anything to be rid of his suffering. Not until the end of the session did Adler indicate that he knew of a means whereby the patient could quickly banish the depression: "The cure is frightfully difficult, one might say drastic. So there is probably no point in my mentioning it to you." Naturally the patient pressed all the more eagerly to know what this cure entailed. Finally Adler allowed himself to be persuaded and explained: "You can be healed if every day you begin first thing in the morning to consider how you can bring a real joy to someone else. If you can stick to this for two weeks you will no longer need therapy."

This sounds positively sentimental, like a Boy Scout ideal, but Adler was no do-gooder. What may strike the reader as disappointingly simple and superficial is in truth powerful stuff. Just as in most instances the act of suicide represents revenge, persistent depression that interferes with one's own life as well as that of others constitutes a masked form of violence as well as an escape hatch for one afraid of the inescapable demands of living with others. The depressed individual cannot think of someone else so intensely that he forgets himself and his own condition. If he should succeed, however, it would be a sign that he wanted to end that condition. He would be taking a step back into active life. In such a case nothing is as healing as concentration on the suffering and the needs of another person, for it allows him, indeed forces him, to give up his dangerous self-preoccupation.

The insight used here therapeutically by Adler is not new; the ancient Chinese philosophers taught that the shortest path to self-knowledge traverses the entire world.

Interlude

FROM A CERTAIN age on, a writer often reacts with total chagrin if not hostile impatience to anything he has just committed to paper. It is with this unsparing self-criticism that one attacks oneself toward the end of the night if one wakes up too early, jolted violently from sleep, usually at the hour when night gives way to morning. The image one receives of oneself in this half-light is a caricature, of course, yet one does not dare to reject it entirely.

In the bright light of day, but in just such a mood, I have reread the first five chapters of this book. I am overwhelmed by doubts: is there any point in writing about psychology? Can I succeed in making the reader familiar with a certain mode of thinking which will in turn allow him to derive some practical knowledge of human nature from his personal experiences?

Knowledge of human nature . . . Everyone deals in it, because every time we meet someone we receive an impression that is transformed into an opinion or a judgment. A writer once said that we carry mirrors through the world to catch its reflection. Yes, but before setting out one paints pictures on large sections of the mirror; it no longer reflects, it deceives.

A method sometimes used to identify criminals describes human faces by means of a series of numbers; a face and its features can be reduced to a code. But even the most mathematically perfect code cannot replace a portrait, cannot render a face. In comparison to the self-portraits of the aging Rembrandt, of poor, unrecognized van Gogh or the resigned Cézanne, the code occupies exactly the same position as experimental psychology, with its mathematically formulated results, does in relation to the psychology of a Shakespeare or a Dostoevsky. The true student of human nature recognizes at a glance the uniqueness of a face and would be able to identify it in a crowd of thousands.

To anyone who has eyes and a clear head, who has not been dazed by illness, every face brings a message either overt or in code. And yet one has the feeling, *I* have the feeling, that it is futile to write about understanding human nature. This doubt makes me wonder how my own understanding of human nature functions. For example, how do I register the message of a face, and why do I sometimes feel the gate to a strange land opening before me? It is the message of loneliness. In the pictures of Edvard Munch one sometimes encounters the cry which must issue from a gaping mouth, but which remains inaudible. That is the silent cry of the lonely, directed at all and at none.

Here I am, writing a book on psychology, a field I turned my back on years ago but could never quite escape from—and yet I do not know what makes an observant human being realize that the person sitting opposite him suffers from the most piercing loneliness, like a prisoner whose guards have left him alone on an endless, snow-covered steppe—alone with fetters on his legs. The fact that a person *can* hear this silent cry is our best clue to his character. Why does this wordless message preoccupy me so intensely?

Let me remind the reader of the refugee child whom I introduced in the Foreword as the later author of this book, the child who had overnight lost everything: the house, the town on the river, the hills of his homeland, the protective shelter of a well-disposed world. He had to flee to strange parts after witnessing the arbitrary destruction of men and animals in the glare of burning houses; and in the great city which he had worshiped from afar he finally experienced a disappointment as searing as personal shame, and had to learn to live with the shattered illusion.

In such loneliness, in the no-man's-land to which one has suddenly been banished, one either succumbs to the unaccustomed fascination of nothingness or one rebels, filled with the desire to change everything. . . .

What is loneliness? In the past, the lonely person was the stranger who was separated by geographical distance from his loved ones, a distance he had temporarily chosen or to which misfortune had consigned him. For thousands of years such isolation provided the initial situation for almost all the great stories and epics. The adventure consisted of the long and perilous way back home; that was true for Joseph and for Ulysses and for all the victors and the vanquished who were lured to strange parts by war. That was true for Don Quixote, Robinson Crusoe, for all the disinherited of history. Loneliness seemed topographically definable: foreign parts were for everyone either enemy territory or a no-man's-land.

Today we see the fear of loneliness in the countless weary faces on the subway near the end of a day in a big city. The subway riders do not feel foreign in their own city, but, squeezed into a narrow space with dozens of others like them, most of whom have the same newspaper in their hands, watch the same television programs—and have done the same the previous evening—each is nevertheless as lonely as a person shipwrecked in the middle of the ocean with only a rotting plank to cling to. This loneliness, which is new and a mass phenomenon, originated in the atmosphere of the metropolis, where from the moment one leaves the house one cannot possibly be alone yet must always remain lonely. However, there is another loneliness which sometimes molds an entire face, which is a mute cry for help, a prison without walls. It results from being cut off, from emotional uprooting, a special kind of homelessness.

A face can reveal all this. What are we to make of this upsetting impression of a loneliness which seems as fateful and incurable as a gnawing disease? Such impressions bring us close to a person even when they seem to be misleading; *seem*—for the person surrounded by many people may still be lonely—and precisely this secret shows in his face.

A second message which reaches us almost as often tells of a sadness that should not be confused with nervous depression. Sometimes it appears in the visage of an acquaintance, a friend. He usually seems lively and gay, but when he is alone and thinks himself unobserved his face assumes an expression which he could seldom discover even in a mirror and then only if he ever showed the mirror anything besides his "mirror face."—for part of the human comedy is that we are performers before the mirror as well as before other people. That is why we observe this sadness more often in unknown passersby than in friends. It does not usually stem from crushing events or disappointments, from sickness or even the death of a loved one; it seems to be unmotivated, not connected with the immediate past or the present. This sadness reveals the true mood of the individual, hidden for hours or days at a time, always returning as soon as the power of the fleeting moment diminishes.

When we are thus shaken by the revelation of another's loneliness or sadness, it is as if something veiled were suddenly bared. Why? Probably because we are stirred by a sympathy that brings us so close to the stranger that we cannot imagine ever not having known him. In this instant he ceases to be a stranger. Through this sympathy, this empathy, we begin to identify with the stranger. We understand him as if he were a part of us or as if we were in his skin. Which comes first: do we identify with him because we feel his loneliness, or do we feel his loneliness because we suddenly identify with him? Unfortunately the sympathy for oneself usually has the greater impact.

You can see what I am getting at: many authors, myself among them, have written hundreds of pages in an attempt to present certain psychological concepts and to impart to the reader a knowledge of human nature. And then—in one of those hours when night gives way to day—the author abruptly realizes that his moments of triumph as a student of human nature were moments in which his intuition took over, when involuntary sympathy, empathy or identification revealed to him the secret of this man with the unhappy face, of this no-longer-young woman: how they spent their days and nights, how the world looked from their point of view and in what state of dissension or misanthropic harmony they lived with themselves.

If this is how it stands, can one actually teach anything? What good are all the descriptions, explanations, interpretations? Elsewhere I have stated, in agreement with many including Adler, that psychology may be a scientific discipline, but at the same time it is other things, and perhaps first and foremost an art. But can this art be taught? To what extent, and how?

I have interrupted myself between the fifth and sixth chapters of this book to let the reader know that this neutral typography conceals not only an author presenting his subject with apparent self-assurance but also another reader: a reader who for reasons of his own knows what is what and is familiar with an author's doubts. And for that reason he knows that one sometimes says more about certain things than one can with complete certainty. Too much and too little: with a few exceptions that formula characterizes every book.

This is not a fit of modesty, which would be misplaced in any case and rather suspect; it is only a reminder that the author and the reader are sitting in the same classroom with the students who have been waiting for an eternity, and in vain, for the teacher who knows everything and can put it into words.

Nietzsche, a philosopher who attacked philosophy and philosophers, said about them and about all psychologists, of whom he was also one:

Every one of them pretends that he has discovered and reached his opinions through the self-development of cold, pure, divinely untroubled dialectic . . . whereas, at bottom, a pre-conceived dogma, a notion, an "institution," or mostly a heart's desire, made abstract and refined, is defended by them with arguments sought after the fact.[1]

By presenting individual psychology and Adler's exceptional part in it, pointing out the elements of self-confession in his teachings, I am doing justice to Nietzsche's welcome principle of analytic doubt. But is it not instructive that one feels attracted by one philosophy or psychology and not by another? One cannot elude the element of confession even if one wants to.

All of this had to be said. But why? If man is not or should not remain a "searing shame," it is up to psychology to give an example of frankness and sincerity. There can be no self-knowledge and no knowledge of human nature without recognition of the limits set for us, and of those barriers which for known or unknown reasons we establish for ourselves and which we alone can remove.

Now I shall interrupt this interlude, itself an interruption, and return to those lonely faces. No one can understand loneliness if he disregards the shadow which non-being casts on being—that is death. No one's imagination, be it ever so lively or creative, could picture the emotional life of a man who knew about death but had the unshakable certainty that he was immune to it for all eternity. The purposiveness without which few of Adler's tenets would be meaningful or even thinkable, this "telemania" tacitly assumes finality, the kind of completion that comes when one reaches a goal; actually the only such completion is death. The purposive person, however, obviously does not realize that it is his own end that awaits him at his destination. When one plans for the future, one expects that beyond every goal another more distant, higher goal beckons, and that every end is merely a stage. In spite of all we know of our short allotted time, of our wretched mortality, we still cherish a wholly unfounded faith in our own durability. We do not *live* death, we only *die* it—yet death

lurks everywhere, in every nook and cranny of our existence.

The loneliness which does not necessarily come from
being alone but can occur in the midst of a crowd is com-
parable only to death. The timelessness the lonely feel is
not the same as the positive timelessness of eternity; rather,
it is time which has reached an end, lack of motion in a gigantic space which has become useless. The sadness of the
lonely person is sorrow for himself; it nourishes the longing for nothingness that overwhelms the person like an
unassuageable homesickness, so that he suddenly and unexpectedly puts an end to his life.

Once more I shall ask why I talk about loneliness so
much. Why have I been thinking for years of writing a
novel whose hero would be an absolutely lonely man adrift
in a city like Vienna? For the same reason that I very early
became a Marxist, a revolutionary who believed that the
world had no right to continue existing unless it underwent
fundamental changes. This I believe to this day. For the
same reason that I turned to psychology and to Adler,
whose diagnostic method seeks to give a scientific basis to
a great promise, the promise of a communal way of life.

This interlude did not turn out quite the way I had intended. I had hoped to say a few words about people who
suffer from their very existence, using such people as an
example to demonstrate that even a psychology concerned
with the loneliest of the lonely cannot help being a study
of society, too. I also meant to suggest why Freudian psychoanalysis could not win over the likes of me—in spite
of its impressive theoretical structure and the fact that I
and many of my contemporaries were attracted by everything in it that challenged bourgeois morality. However,
its founder had little to say about us, and he lost us com-

pletely when, after the horrors of World War I, he felt he could explain the existence of an army by positing a libidinous relationship between the soldiers and their military leaders.

That was about fifty years ago, and the situation has not changed. Nor has my conviction that the world must be transformed by people themselves become changed.

Part Three

Chapter VI

WITH FEW EXCEPTIONS, the creators of interpretive psychotherapy were psychiatrists and neurologists who set out to discover the causes and motivation behind such so-called nervous diseases as hysteria. Among the first and second generation of these researchers, hypnotism was expected to unravel the origins of these diseases and to provide a method for curing them. These doctors were not alone; a broad intellectual public also yielded to the fascination of hypnotism, which was widespread until the end of the nineteenth century. Today it is once again finding adherents.

For thousands of years man was acquainted with a disease which he called hysteria and regarded as a disorder connected with the lower abdomen and occurring only in women. This conception was finally modified in the second half of the nineteenth century, and then tended to be recognized as a nervous illness which had little or no connection with the female genital organs. In Paris and Nancy psychiatrists supported by psychologists like Pierre Janet dared to diagnose hysteria as an essentially emotional disorder. They sought its origins in certain emotional and mental processes which were unconscious or barely conscious and often produced mental leaps, the formation of illogical ideas and depressive states of anxiety. All of these manifestations appeared now as cause, now as effect. Thanks to exploratory hypnosis, the French psychiatrists succeeded in discovering experiences which the patients had forgotten or whose importance became evident only in the context that could be established with information obtained while the patient was under hypnosis.

Charcot was much ridiculed when he presented his hypnotic cases at the Salpêtrière. He was reproached for turning his lectures and demonstrations into theatrical spectacles which attracted a sensation-hungry audience. Today no one denies that we owe to this researcher and to Pierre Janet the creation of a new psychopathology and with it a new type of man-centered science which has made its mark on the whole world despite enormous resistance. One of the most respectful and eager of Charcot's listeners was Sigmund Freud. In the autumn of 1885 he wrote his future wife enthusiastic letters describing Charcot as one of the greatest doctors and as a sober man of genius who was destroying Freud's own cherished opinions and objectives. He wondered whether this seed would bear fruit. But he knew that no human being had impressed him as profoundly as Charcot. Freud's own research on hysteria undertaken with Breuer was later to yield results that were of immense importance for the further development of psychopathology and the study of neurosis.

But here we are primarily interested in the background against which psychopathology was to establish itself, particularly in Central Europe. The new way of looking at things never really took root in Charcot's homeland. Psychotherapy has never achieved the position in France that it has in Protestant countries, in England and especially in the United States, where the influx of psychologists of all schools in the 1930s helped make psychotherapy part of the national way of life.

Treatment of the emotionally disturbed based on the theory of psychogenesis was for many years a Viennese specialty. And far out of proportion to their percentage of the population it was Jews who took advantage of it. Another factor is even more crucial: in contrast to the patients whom Charcot and other psychiatrists treated in clinics and hospitals, the psychotherapists' patients belonged to the affluent or culturally advantaged classes. So from the outset the new method was reserved for a socially defined group, not on principle but for practical economic reasons. The situation has been somewhat improved today, due to the increasing use of group therapy, but private treatment is still the privilege of the affluent.

One may say without exaggeration that because of this state of affairs psychotherapists of all schools have derived their insights and experiences from a narrow social milieu. It may be useful to examine some of the attitudes of the upper and middle classes during these years, the last phase of bourgeois good conscience in Europe. For example, everyone accepted the notion that women of these classes needed special indulgence during their menstrual period. Parts of the house had to be kept dark, noise had to be avoided or muted. During a woman's "period" one had no claims whatsoever on her; she was dispensed from all exertion. At the same time one took it for granted that other women, particularly servants, were in no way hindered by menstruation; they were not physically weakened or less able to work and in need of indulgence. Likewise it was unthinkable, indeed downright ludicrous, that a woman of the people should complain of nerves. Nerves began at a certain class or income level. Nerves in every form: sensitivity to noise, being indisposed for no apparent reason, minor but melodramatic fainting fits, susceptibility of the senses, especially that of smell, and delicacy of heart and stomach—all these were characteristic attributes of a woman of the upper classes. It is hardly believable and yet indubitably true that emphasis on the social differences between the aristocrat and the citizen in seventeenth-century Paris was subtler and less obvious than the line of division between the working classes, the so-called people, and the "better" classes in the second half of the nineteenth century.

If one reads carefully the cases discussed by Freud, Adler, Jung, Stekel and many of their colleagues and pupils, one can establish that although the number of patients from the lower middle class rose significantly in the course of time, the percentage of proletarian cases remained as tiny as the percentage of university students from proletarian households. Lest I be misunderstood: this reference should by no means be considered a reproach directed at psychotherapists or as a hint at their class snobbery or greed. Neither the reproach nor the hint would be justified. The entire socioeconomic situation was such that even the specific morbid awareness attained by neurotic, emotionally disturbed ladies and gentlemen was out of the question for the people. They suffered, too, of course, but they had no right to indulge their illness or to use it to achieve neurotic ends. Even within the family they were denied solicitude.

At issue here is not a foolish accusation such as an eager revolutionary would make, but consequences resulting from an objective set of circumstances: since these psychotherapists dealt mainly with patients from a certain class, with characteristic values, prejudices, personality ideals, educational methods and adaptive requirements, they studied the modes of behavior, the manners and the techniques which were current within this class. For most of the patients absence or loss of property was of great moment, so that all relationships intended to last, not least of all marriage, were made or broken by the prospects for maintaining or adding to property.

The clientele of the psychotherapists was, I said, bourgeois, very often Jewish. Among Catholics, confession offers considerable competition for any kind of mental therapy; even apart from its religious function it can be very effective. Though catharsis may not be sufficient as a means of psychological liberation—of this Breuer and Freud became convinced when treating their hysteria patients—it can still help the sufferer over many a difficult situation.

Protestants have no confession, and Jews must not only forgo this but also all mediation between man and God. That is one of the reasons why Jews were not only among the founders and pioneers of the "Jewish science" but also well represented among its patients. (This was especially true in Austria-Hungary.) There are more important reasons for this state of affairs which relate not only to the Jews' religion but to their social situation. We shall return to this point later.

Let me mention a "deviation" which once held an enormous importance for some of my generation, me included, and which may become relevant again for the present younger generation. This deviation was unquestionably the primary factor in Adler's seeing the break with me as unavoidable; he brought it about in the interests of the future of individual psychology. When we Marxist individual psychologists—Alice and Otto Rühle, myself and others —began forty years ago to analyze these social factors critically, we had no idea of disparaging "bourgeois" psychology, let alone Adler's teaching; in fact we used Adler's work as a point of reference. We wanted to investigate the relationship between general economic and social relations on the one hand, and individual problems, on the other. Furthermore we considered it necessary to examine thoroughly to what extent and how one could proceed from individual psychology to a social characterology. We did not assert that we would create a Marxist psychology.

These debates began around 1925, and became vehement disputes after the outbreak of the world economic crisis, when millions of the unemployed suffered unspeakable misery and degradation; no wonder they became bitter. Many of us worked as psychological consultants in welfare and public relief agencies and with the juvenile courts. The nonbourgeois clientele of the child guidance clinics was already familiar to most Adlerians, but we now encountered conditions, facts and problems that one seldom met with in private practice.

During those years this Marxist-inspired deviation gained influence not only among individual psychologists but also among psychoanalysts. This deeply disturbed orthodox adherents of all schools. At this time the final break came between Freud and Wilhelm Reich, who, unlike Herbert Marcuse, pushed ahead with a consistency that shunned compromise, roundly rejecting sublimation and arriving via the "sex pole" at his famous theory of orgasm.

Around this time, when Stalin's total victory was just in the offing, liquidation of modern interpretive psychology began in the Soviet Union; psychoanalysis as well as individual psychology were banned there as in the Third Reich.

It can be readily understood that in those catastrophic years the proper milieu of the interpretive psychologist and the psychotherapist, the family, seemed unbearably narrow. We often asked ourselves whether we were wasting our time patching the plaster while the house had been set on fire and was threatening to collapse.

It was in keeping with Freud's basic concept of man to analyze him in his most intimate family relations—and mostly retrospectively. Society was regarded as a giant extension of the family, with patricidal complexes and libidinous or incestuous fixations; history was a *chronique scandaleuse familiale*. Freud's works *Totem and Taboo* and *Mass Psychology and Ego-Analysis*, although written after the World War I and the Russian Revolution, give eloquent expression to this conception. On the basis of his views on the community and social interest, and probably under the influence of Marxism, Adler saw the family only as a historically mutable form of the community. Nevertheless he could not resist the temptation to concentrate his interest primarily on the family, on what creates it, what destroys it, and what in it produces neurosis.

Adler was neither the first nor the only person to recognize nervous disorders as a societal, an asocial and antisocial, phenomenon. But earlier and with more precision than others he defined neurosis as a social phenomenon and formulated a goal for treatment which today is accepted by psychotherapists of almost every persuasion, even if their separate jargons conceal their basic agreement. In the volume of collected studies, *The Practice and Theory of Individual Psychology* (which appeared in German in 1920), Adler says:

The path of the neurosis does not lead in the direction of social functioning, nor does it aim at solving given life-problems but finds an outlet for itself in the small family circle, thus achieving the isolation of the patient.

The larger unit of the social group is either completely or very extensively pushed aside by a mechanism consisting of hyper-sensitiveness and intolerance. Only a small group is left over for the maneuvers aiming at the various types of superiority to expend themselves upon. At the same time protection and the withdrawal from the demands of the community and the decisions of life are made possible.

Thus estranged from reality, the neurotic man lives a life of imagination and phantasy and employs a number of devices for enabling him to side-step the demands of reality and for reaching out toward an ideal situation which would free him from any service for the community and absolve him from responsibility.

These exemptions and the privileges of illness and suffering give him a substitute for his original hazardous goal of superiority.

Thus the neurosis and the psyche represent an attempt to free oneself from all the constraints of the community by establishing a counter-compulsion. This latter is so constituted that it effectively faces the peculiar nature of the surroundings and their demands. Both of those convincing inferences can be drawn from the manner in which this counter-compulsion manifests itself and from the neuroses selected.

The counter-compulsion takes on the nature of a revolt, gathers its material either from favorable affective experiences or from observations. It permits thoughts and affects to become preoccupied either with the above-mentioned stirrings or with unimportant details, as long as they at least serve the purpose of directing the eye and the attention of the patient away from his life-problems. In this manner, depending upon the needs of the situation, he prepares anxiety- and compulsion-situations, slightly pathological affects, neurasthenic and hypochondriacal complexes and psychotic pictures of his actual condition, all of which are to serve him as excuses.

Even logic falls under the domination of the counter-compulsion. As in psychosis this process may go as far as the actual nullification of logic.

Logic, the will to live, love, human sympathy, co-operation and language, all arise out of the needs of human communal life. Against the latter are directed automatically all the plans of the neurotic individual striving for isolation and lusting for power.

To cure a neurosis and a psychosis it is necessary to change completely the whole up-bringing of the patient and turn him definitely and unconditionally back upon human society.[1]

Insofar as the human being is "an ensemble of social conditions," his emotional disorders are clearly an expression of an actual (i.e., not fictional or pretended) relation to the special conditions he must actively or passively adapt to. The neurotic, who is likely to seek the impossibly absolute from his family, protests against the demands of society and uses illness to force his family to accede to his demands. But his behavior, a continuous failure, affects both his close relatives and wider circles; it acts as a constant sabotage. Here is a case history that illustrates this mechanism:

Twenty years ago Mrs. C., who came from a poor family, met a wealthy man who fell in love with her extraordinary beauty and married her. For a long time she lived in fear that the gradual decline of her physical attractiveness would weaken her position vis-à-vis her husband and his family. She developed an increasing distrust of her husband, until finally she had reason to suspect that he had acquired a very pretty young mistress. Shortly thereafter her agoraphobia broke out. She was absolutely incapable of taking one step outside her house unless accompanied by her husband. And since she could never predict when she would have the energy to go out, even when her husband went with her, he always had to be at her disposal, ready to break off his work at the drop of a hat, to be called away from appointments, to cancel planned trips. He had to give up trying to arrange anything in advance. Frustrated, the man finally gave up his office and broke with his mistress.

At one time there were many such cases, but the number has diminished appreciably, because of the same changes that have made hysteria all but extinct in the technologically advanced countries, where it appears only now and then as a provincial phenomenon. One still finds it in primitive countries, and there primarily among the affluent. Where the situation of women, especially their style of life, has undergone fundamental change, the melodrama of the menstrual period has also gone out of fashion, and with it the concomitant manifestations that tended to promote neurosis. The professional and social life of women is, with a few exceptions, no longer disrupted by it. Thus the lady and her maid, the woman director of a large company and her filing clerk have become equals. Nerves and migraines have ceased to be marks of privilege. Not that new medications have been discovered, although the use of drugs has been increased at all levels of the population by the availability of health-care plans. To parody the language of the fashion reporters, one might say that "they are no longer wearing" hysteria, ostentatious nervousness, feminine helplessness and the propensity to swoon. This change is one of the numerous consequences of that far-reaching transformation in manners and life styles which directly followed World War I. It is not a consequence of psychological enlightenment, psychoanalysis, individual psychology and other branches, nor of modern educational methods.

To return to Mrs. C. with her agoraphobia and the total victory Mrs. C. won by accepting personal defeat in the form of anxiety and an inability to live like others: she subdued her husband more thoroughly with her agoraphobia than she had previously done with her youth, and her beauty. A woman might still accomplish this today, but doubtless with much more difficulty than sixty years ago. It would be more difficult, partly because of the changed attitude of the affluent toward their professional work. In the course of the past half-century, work has ceased to be a disgrace—earlier it had been so undesirable in certain circles that a proverb had to emphasize that "work is no disgrace." Today on the other hand there exists a general work ethic which is stressed in the education of even the most privileged children. In Europe the man of leisure, the dandy, the happy-go-lucky pensioner have all become rarities, lounging around unnoticed. Today a husband would hardly be expected to jeopardize his professional position by submitting to a neurotic wife; he would see to it that she received psychotherapeutic attention, preferably with a period spent in an appropriate institution. She would have to reconcile herself to being accompanied by a nurse or an aide, paid to do the job. Neurosis is today recognized as a legitimate illness by medical insurance plans, but its fundamentally asocial character nowadays causes the sick person's relatives to shun him more than they used to; they want to escape the destructive sabotage that an acute neurosis can produce.

The neurotic "encounter-compulsion" of which Adler speaks is usually a passive but highly effective protest against the pressure exerted by the community to make the individual bow to certain necessities, accept compromises and adjust to this or that unpleasantness. Very useful diagnostic conclusions can be drawn from the forms of counter-compulsion with which the neurotic responds to his milieu and its demands. Adler's seemingly simple techniques are actually based on a deep knowledge of human nature and prove especially useful. Here is one technique which everyone should apply to himself from time to time:

Confronted with disturbances like agoraphobia or claustrophobia or neurotic compulsions which interfered with normal daily life, Adler used to ask himself, "What would the sick person have had to do if these disorders had not disabled him?" In order to answer this sort of question one has to study the immediate circumstances of the patient, including even seemingly inconsequential details. Only this exact investigation allows one to explain the "neurotic arrangement," as Adler called it. One then discovers how and to what extent neurosis is a special method of life adapted to "private logic."

Let us return once more to the case of Mrs. C. If what we have here is really an unconscious but calculated arrangement, we should ask what this woman would have had to do if she had been spared this phobia. In her determination to defend her position, she would have had to take up the struggle against her rival and force her husband to confess to his infidelity and renounce his mistress. But Mrs. C. knew that she did not have the weapons necessary for an open conflict, for she had lost these along with her youth. She owed the most important success of her life to her beauty and attractiveness. That her husband was able to deceive her proved that another woman was now exercising an equally irresistible attraction. To be sure, at the onset of her marital crisis Mrs. C. had attempted to restore her appeal, using the pathetic but tried-and-true stratagems women have always resorted to, but her efforts had gone unrewarded. She concluded that her husband was not to be won back in this way, so she chose the opposite course. If she could not be the triumphant Venus, she would have to elicit sympathy by transforming herself into a miserable sufferer. If her husband left her in the lurch, he would reveal to the whole world that he was abandoning her because she was ill and because he felt greater loyalty for a little no-good.

One would say that this was a very clever move by Mrs. C., for she risked nothing and stood to gain everything. By acting much more helpless than she really was, she won back the superior position which her youth and beauty had provided earlier. But a very simple fact speaks against this interpretation; Mrs. C.'s acquaintances would have attested without the slightest hesitation that this woman was possessed of a very mediocre intelligence, and furthermore she had never been distinguished by any cunning to speak of. Is it not remarkable, is it indeed at all believable, that she would have chosen such a wily form of combat? The answer is obvious: her choice was not conscious, or at most only partially conscious.

Anxiety is an easy emotion to whip up in oneself, for each of us is acquainted with it from earliest childhood, even if it seldom comes to the fore. The constant fear of losing her husband to another woman, the terrible prospect of being totally diminished in his eyes, created anxiety in Mrs. C., the feeling of being exposed to unknown perils.

It is not difficult to feign anxiety states, but even a talented actor would hardly be able to keep up the pretense over a period of days or weeks. So it was in fact better that this agoraphobia, though neurotically arranged, should seem to strike Mrs. C. suddenly and unexpectedly. For someone who has been neglected or ignored during childhood, it is difficult to use illness as a refuge, as a defense against danger, or, as Adler would say, as a trusty counter-compulsion against the pressures of those around one who have become less assiduous in their care, affection and attention. Everyone knows that families try to make up for the discomfort of illness by showing extra solicitude. One is rewarded for illness: this is the experience of coddled children, and it stays with them even after they have become fathers or grandfathers. Such was also the case with Mrs. C. In her day, part of the superior male role was to provide protection for women and to accompany them wherever discomfort threatened or they might suffer distress. In the spirit of Hegelian dialectics, these men became the slaves of their slaves. In a similar situation a working-class wife would hardly have sought refuge in agoraphobia. If she had, she would have completely ruined her marriage and probably caused the economic collapse of the family. It was of course out of the question for a working-class man to stop work or to interrupt it merely to accompany his wife on her errands. Among the unpropertied classes one often encountered such agoraphobia in young girls and in widows, who called on the services of a son, a daughter or a granddaughter as a way of escaping terrible loneliness and securing at least for a few hours some tender attention. All too often such devious efforts ended in humiliating failures, which under some circumstances produced paranoia.

The characteristic cases treated by the various schools of psychotherapy during their first decades were sociologically quite homogeneous. But that is not the chief point to be made. Psychoneurosis has always existed, and in all social groups, although its specific manifestations and forms of expression have varied according to historical conditions, the social system, and the *Zeitgeist*. In terms of social psychology, it is a very important fact that neurosis was not recognized as an independent psychogenetic illness until the second half of the nineteenth century, and that it was not generally acknowledged until this century. Before that time emotional disorder and the organic dysfunctions which went along with them were regarded either as the secondary symptoms of various diseases, usually misdiagnosed, or as the charming emotional quirks of particularly sensitive, finely made individuals. An example would be depression, which was poetically termed "melancholy" and could frequently be observed in the well-studied poses struck by romantic lovers. In the eighteenth century people wept freely; tears were proof of genuineness of feeling.

Neurosis has been regarded as a curable illness for only the past one hundred years. One might assume that this fact can be attributed simply to scientific progress. The history of medicine seems to speak for this interpretation: modern research methods presently make possible the diagnosis and successful treatment of illnesses that once went unsuspected or were mistaken for something else. Without excluding this possibility entirely, one may still insist that neurosis represents a special case. One can easily demonstrate that it has been known for centuries, if not for millennia; its amazingly late recognition cannot be ascribed to lack of the psychological insights that have become available only recently. The rapid development of psychopathology as well as the new social and medical attitude toward neurosis are both due to recent upheavals in social relations, including the radical change in the role of the family. Previously the family constituted the decisive personal framework within which the individual was shaped and enabled to adjust to life. Generation followed generation with only minimal variations. (Every family had a certain percentage of "black sheep" who were never mentioned.) Left to "rot behind bars." In general, however, the family remained stable, its aim to bring forth more people "like us." Social mobility was so slight that parish and community records show both urban and rural families following the same patterns for hundreds of years. It was reasonable to view adaptation to the world, the most important objective in child-rearing, as identical with adaptation to the home, to family life.

By opening up new, seemingly inexhaustible sources of energy, industrial society created a growing mobility: migration from the country to the city took on vast dimensions; with this went the loosening and often destruction of family ties. Within the urban population this mobility became a factor in social and economic betterment, also facilitated by the tremendous increase in production of consumer goods for mass consumption. On the one hand we witnessed constant economic improvement within all social strata, and on the other hand the profound and disruptive transformations that go with large-scale class mobility. There was also a steady increase in the size of those population groups engaged in technical, intellectual, organizational, administrative and commercial functions. At the same time the institutes of higher learning opened their doors to ever more sudents. The barriers which once separated the classes and made upward mobility difficult have still not disappeared entirely, but their negative influence has palpably diminished.

In the course of the complex and far-reaching process, the improbable happened: expulsion from the paradise of the family, that Eden which often constituted a private hell. The family, far from remaining an unassailable bulwark, came to need protection, for its countless claims to authority, its rules, customs, manners, private obsessions and taboos began to lose their immediate relevance. The hold of the family relaxed, but what remained was as burdensome as ever. This twilight of the gods will continue a long time, perhaps forever, because the family is unlikely to become totally expendable, at least as long as human life begins at point zero and needs help in moving to more advanced stages.

This change in the function of the family and its obvious disintegration produced in the Jewish middle class, especially that of Central Europe, a sudden feeling of nakedness. As is the case with all persecuted minorities, the family among Jews was an especially strong bulwark; all the setbacks, vexations and disappointments which a Jewish child experienced in the outside world were compensated for by an excess of tenderness on the part of his relatives. This explains why Jews made up such a large proportion of psychotherapy patients at the turn of the century. They were seeking first of all, a cure for their suffering, but also a new, much-needed extra-familial bulwark. They were delighted with the assurance they received from the therapist that their family experiences could be interpreted in an entirely new fashion and that one could achieve emotional independence of the family without having to feel ungrateful or disloyal—that in fact such independence was a must.

In the past, the best possible adaptation to the immediate environment had consisted in the son's following in his father's footsteps. In modern industrial society, however, the urban family has ceased to be a production unit and is merely a consuming unit. Social mobility in the early twentieth century was accompanied by continual reshuffling of professions. One's profession no longer required adaptation to family tradition but integration into a new social milieu in which emotional claims no longer made themselves heard.

This revolution accounts for the increase in the number of cases of serious social maladjustment. Although feminine neurosis no longer took the melodramatic form of hysteria, it represented an increasing threat to marriage and family life. Unlike their mothers and their grandmothers, twentieth-century women acknowledged their sexuality and became resentful of the comedy of love which played itself out after a few years of marriage in lovelessness and sexual indifference on the part of the male.

The demand for happiness in life was first legitimized and universalized by the eighteenth-century bourgeois revolution, becoming part of its revolutionary liturgy. But not until the twentieth century has happiness become a practical demand in the battle of the classes, the generations and the sexes. This demand finally prevailed against the inhibitions long effectively imposed on love life by moralistic upbringing. It was no longer enough to marry a "provider," to bear and raise children; it was more important to find a real partner and with him the happiness of loving and being loved. This may be one of the reasons for the decline in cases of hysteria: the hysterical woman took pains to conceal from herself her longing for emotional and often physical gratification and the nagging discontent caused in her by marriage and family life. She staged a long drama full of sensational turnabouts, less in order to change her situation—she lacked the courage for that—than to indulge herself in an intensity which life failed to provide, and to obtain unlimited sympathy and an unassailable position of superiority within the family. Twenty or thirty years later her daughter the neurotic sought out the psychotherapist, concealed her neurosis from no one and uninhibitedly and exhaustively reported on her sexual experiences—from a first encounter with an exhibitionist and childhood sexplay to adulterous leanings, temptations, and finally marital infidelity.

Even these breakthroughs are today already part of history, as are the assertions of so many philosophers, priests and doctors that woman is by nature a modest creature and, if normal, unsensual and therefore naturally frigid. This modesty no longer exists, or at least women feel it no more than men, perhaps less. And of course the modern woman decidedly rejects moral pressures calculated to make her frigid. Masculine protest, which formerly used frigidity as an effective means of evading the feminine role, now expresses itself in the opposite fashion; women aggressively seek sexual adventure, attempting to equal the feats of male Don Juans.

Up to this point we have been discussing neurotics who slyly gain various advantages for themselves by means of tricks, stratagems, arrangements, elaborate excuses and finally flight into illness. Is it not true then that patients seek out the psychiatrist or therapist primarily because they are suffering, because their lives are made miserable by anxiety, nervous compulsions, depression and so many other torments characteristic of neurosis, not the least of which are functional disorders that attack sensitive, congenitally inferior organs? These patients are usually seeking happiness by circuitous routes which often turn out to be dead ends. But isn't the important point that they want to free themselves of the misery to which illness has condemned them—even when they themselves have arranged their sickness?

Regardless of the social preconditions that made the early neurotics relatively homogeneous, then as now it was a matter of human beings who were suffering because they created suffering—their own and that of their loved ones. In discussions revolving around this point, for example in conversations with patients who did not want to believe in neurotic arrangement because they realized they would have to face up to the existence of their own stratagems, and to free themselves from them, Adler liked to answer objections with the comment, "Well, what do you expect —to accomplish all that, to mess up so much and still be happy?" He often told the anecdote of a Budapest counterfeiter who succeeded in reproducing silver crown pieces so accurately that no specialists could distinguish the real from the fake. "And although the man could not be caught and in fact never was, he gave up counterfeiting of his own free will. You see," Adler added, "to produce one crown cost him one crown twenty-five."

The excessive cost, the ruinous cost to himself describes the suffering of the neurotic; this is how he pays for the success of his arrangements: the subjugation of his patients, his wife, his children, or the privilege of passing his days in idleness, of letting himself go, of binding himself to a woman he does not love and torturing her with mad jealousy, or demanding compassion while withholding it from others.

Should one conclude that no one can create suffering for others without also bringing it down on himself? Should one compare the neurotic to a prisoner who is chained to a fellow prisoner and cannot push him away without injuring himself? One can refuse to share one's life with one's fellow human beings, but one cannot elude them. This fact kindles the suspicion that life—in God's image—proves much more reliable in doling out punishments than in offering rewards.

Chapter VII

PSYCHOSOMATIC THERAPY, which may soon replace psychotherapy, is without question the oldest form of treatment for human suffering. Magicians, medicine men and priests have used it from time immemorial to cure illnesses of all kinds. Civilized travelers who found this method in use among primitive peoples ridiculed it, but they were ridiculing themselves without realizing it.

The magical conception of illness rests principally on the supposition that the individual is subject to certain influences that he has unwittingly created through deeds or omissions. It is chiefly a matter of the ominous but unavoidable clashes that result from cohabitation of the living with the spirits of their tribal ancestors. Illness would thus be the consequences of a discord between a spirit and a living person. The sick person is then no longer himself; robbed of his own will, he becomes the property of a hostile spirit, who has taken possession of his body and soul. Thus possessed, he is snatched from the present and incorporated partially or wholly into the past, the realm of the dead. The magic healer proceeds to identify the evil spirit, to reconcile him with the victim or to drive him out by other means. From the point of view of animistic medicine, every illness is alienation in the true sense of the word. The magician attempts to uncover the secret which the sick person unknowingly carries within him like a deadly poison. If the treatment does not succeed in bringing the patient to himself, he succumbs to the power of the dead, who snatch him out of life for good.

The difference between this magical conception and the basic tenets of modern psychotherapy is not great, which becomes evident as soon as one gets past the barrier of professional jargon. The psychotheraphist as much as the magician is convinced that he must free his patient from the weight of the past. He must therefore make the patient so conscious of the past that he almost experiences it a second time. Hence the process of bringing-to-consciousness must be regarded as all-important. All questions of technique—the use of free association, interpretation of dreams and childhood recollections, the more or less active role the therapist assumes, i.e., his overt or covert intervention or his passivity—are secondary by comparison.

Unlike other psychologists, including Freud, Adler believed that the psychotherapist should be an educator who actively helped his patients in their self-education or re-education. The therapist who sits, unseen, behind a patient stretched out on a couch and appears to be totally neutral conforms to the orthodox psychoanalytical conception, but has no part in Adlerian psychotherapy. To the individual psychologist this is not only a ridiculously transparent act, but also a pointless impediment to contact. The psychoanalyist of course once specifically wanted to impede contact, if not eliminate it altogether at times. That practice has largely been dropped nowadays. Significant changes have taken place in psychoanalytic method during the last two decades, thanks to the work of Dr. F. Alexander among others. It is becoming increasingly similar to Adlerian therapy, but unfortunately this fact has not been acknowledged by any revisions in theory. One can speak here of an immense victory for individual psychology, a victory Adler foresaw; he also predicted that decades would pass before psychoanalysts would admit he had been right all along.

No statistics exist on the patients undergoing psychoanalysis fifty years ago, right after the end of the First World War, and we also do not know the number of patients under treatment today. But there can be no doubt that the number has greatly increased, as has the number of psychotherapists. We must include psychological group therapy, which was practically unknown in Adler's day. Today patients who cannot afford private treatment vastly outnumber those who can. Group therapy requires certain modifications in the method of treatment, in particular in the manner of bringing-to-consciousness. There are compelling reasons for the assumption that the collective, easily varied method is gaining steadily in importance, especially in large cities.

In the past, opponents of the various schools of psychotherapy came up with a variety of objections. They insisted that psychological treatment consisted merely of conversations in which one partner, whether talkative or taciturn, always occupied center stage. How could mere conversation produce a healing effect? the detractors asked. In the course of time this skeptical reproach has given way to another concern which is the basic premise of all interpretive psychotherapy: the existence and influence of the unconscious. Behaviorists firmly reject the idea of the unconscious; representatives of most schools of experimental psychology take a similar, fundamentally critical position. They will accept what can be proven, tested and verified. For "purely scientific reasons" they refuse to acknowledge the unconscious; they assert it cannot be located by their methods or pinpointed in experience. Adler, who certainly did not question the usefulness of tests and regarded with interest some of the research methods and results of experimental psychology, once used the following example to refute the experimentalists' standards of verification:

A man has holed up in a fortress surrounded by a high, thick wall and a deep moat. The entrance to this abode is known to him alone. Electric warning devices prevent anyone from straying in. All the window panes are made of bullet-proof glass and covered with double bars and steel shutters which only he can open and close. The guards are observed by other guards, who in turn are guarded and whose families can at any time be arrested as hostages. The man has fully provided for his security.

Now our lord of the fortress lies down on his couch to read, alternating between horror stories and detective novels, smoking cigarettes made especially for him, drinking whiskey and eating pralines. If an experimental psychologist were invited in, he would be unable to find any trace of fear or anxiety in the man, even using the most advanced and sensitive measuring apparatus.

And yet each of this man's security measures is clearer evidence than any confession; more than trembling hands or chattering teeth they prove that the master of this fortress is dominated by a thousand terrors and fears. One can state this even though examination may clearly reveal that the man's pulse rate is normal, that his breathing is regular, that his hand does not shake when he puts a glass, a cigarette or a fork to his mouth, that he has an excellent appetite and sleeps soundly.

This example shows that certain psychologists know less about human nature than a lonely shepherd in an Alpine meadow. It also reminds us that scientific isolation of modes of behavior may cause such a false impression of the subject, man, that he vanishes before our very eyes, even if the scientific methods used are unimpeachable.

Yet apart from the objections mentioned here, the question as to the verifiable success or failure of psychotherapeutic treatment or any kind of therapy is thoroughly justified. Over seventy years have passed since psychotherapy dispensed with hypnosis, suggestion and the cathartic methods of the early days and made extension of consciousness almost its exclusive method—and goal. Psychoneurotic analysis had led to the conclusion that certain matters need only be brought to the patient's awareness for him to be cured, or at least for the basis, the purpose, the motive of his illness to disappear. As was logical, given this particular method of treatment, it was not until surprisingly late, about twenty-five years ago, that serious and methodical studies of its results were undertaken. Research and comparative studies were finally devoted to the individual branches of psychotherapy and to all other kinds of therapy, as well as to the development of cases that were under observation but not treatment. I believe I can assert, without doing anyone an injustice, that among the doctors and psychologists who led these inquiries, quite a few were ready to welcome findings that cast a bad light on interpretive psychotherapy. Many joined the investigations because they were convinced that they would discover what they were looking for. It is true, however, that their findings and comparisons now enable us to form an opinion on the relative success of psychotherapy. I believe one must formulate such an opinion with great caution and many qualifications.

All the researchers involved sought to arrive at universally acceptable definitions of neurosis and of attempted, achieved or unsuccessful cure. They further hoped to differentiate among the various cases on the basis of particular characteristics, the severity of each disorder, its duration and the degree to which it had been neglected. It was unanimously agreed that no psychotherapist treats his patients using merely his own ideas and personal experience, but employs a selective combination of theories. Orthodox psychoanalysts of the Freudian school and a few others tend to adhere more strictly to one theory. Regardless of what theory of genesis and development of neurosis is applied, and regardless of the techniques chosen by individual therapists, in every case one can speak of a cure or significant improvement only if the following behavioral goals can be shown to have been achieved:

1. A return to work, and the ability to behave at work and in the management of life in accordance with the dictates of necessary social adjustment, and this without interruption for at least five years following treatment.

2. An end to complaining of essentially subjective difficulties and disorders.

3. Successful social adaptation.

I quote the above guidelines from Hans J. Eysenck, the well-known British psychologist, whose studies on the effects of psychotherapy attracted much attention and everywhere sparked lively and often fruitful debate.[1]

These guidelines correspond in general to Adler's teaching, which judges a person's capacity for life in society by the degree to which he is able to fulfill the following three life tasks:

1. The social task of active, flexible adaptation to society.

2. The task of pursuing a socially useful activity especially one's work or a profession.

3. The task of being a partner, of loving and receiving love.

Eysenck surveyed all those studies that were based on verifiable comparisons. He compared groups of similar cases; one group had been treated psychotherapeutically; another with chemical or physical means, but primarily with the age-old, seldom-mentioned prescription of rest or recuperation in clinics or convalescent homes; and finally a third group of patients whose illness was diagnosed but not treated. What follows are some of the results Eysenck summarizes, results arrived at after innumerable studies and a long testing period and shown to be reliable and verifiable. Of Eysenck's eight major conclusions we shall mention the four that seem most relevant in this connection.

1. In a comparison of test groups of untreated neurotics with groups of patients who received psychotherapeutic treatment, it was found that the number of cures or major improvements in both groups was about equal.

2. Neurotics who were treated psychotherapeutically recovered or experienced improvement in their condition in the same proportion as neurotics who underwent some other form of treatment.

3. The patients of psychoanalysts made no more rapid progress than those treated by therapists of other schools or by eclectics.

4. Learning therapy achieved much more rapid progress than psychoanalysis or other kinds of psychotherapy.

Eysenck's summary may seem very discouraging, but it should not be grounds for pessimism, since he himself, like most of the authors he quotes, sets quite high the percentage of those considered cured on the basis of the abovementioned criteria: depending on the particular study, cures range between fifty and seventy per cent, although to be sure the same success was achieved with other means of treatment and even with no treatment at all; the outcome was recorded two years after diagnosis of the illness or after the beginning of treatment.

To what degree can or must one accept as definitive these investigations and the conclusions I have sketched here? Before we turn to this question, we must weigh a few fundamental considerations. But first one observation: why, one wonders, did so many years pass before the effectiveness of psychotherapy was subjected to methodical scrutiny, using not just theory but comparative statistics? It is always difficult to say just how effective a method of treatment is, unless one is talking about surgery or the use of specific pharmaceutical preparations. We all know how the chemical industry continues to market more and more pain-killers, products distinguishable more by their brand names than by variations in their ingredients. Doctors try these drugs, replace an old and too familiar medication with a new one on which their patients can pin more hopes. Initially the doctors are not disappointed. Similar effects are achieved with placebos. Thus the effect of a medicine, a treatment, a new method of healing cannot be readily established with much objectivity. The subjective attitude of the suffering patient is an objectively more important and at times decisive factor—when the chief concern is not so much to cure the disease as to give the sufferer a feeling of improvement, of renewed hope. If this is true for organic disorders, is it not even more true of every kind of emotional suffering? One can agree with E. Bleuler, the eminent but little-recognized Swiss psychiatrist, who speaks of the beneficial effects of *udenotherapy;* he uses this Greek-derived term for something that figured prominently in Eysenck's investigations: nontreatment. Here is an example which may be typical of many situations:

A man no longer young whose fiancée had died of a serious illness shortly before they were to be married had withdrawn more and more into himself, and soon began to develop the characteristic traits of an aging bachelor. He lived as if he needed no one, as if he expected no help from anyone, and as if he owed nothing to anybody. His doctor finally insisted that he spend his vacation at a health resort. It happened that on the very first day of his stay he rescued another guest whose life was in danger. News of his courageous intervention spread immediately, and all were certain that he was a well-meaning and helpful man who intentionally but clumsily tried to conceal that fact. At first he wanted to dispel this impression, but he did not do so energetically enough, for, naturally, he enjoyed this unexpected and unaccustomed public approbation. And gradually he grew into a role that had never been his before. He became everyone's favorite vacation companion and was welcome at all the intimate parties. When he went home he was no longer alone in the big city, for most of the other vacationers also lived there. From then on he belonged to a group of people who were happy to see him and who trusted him. They had all given this joyless man psychic treatment, without of course suspecting it. By placing certain expectations on him they had helped him more than they could ever guess. Is this a case of Bleuler-style udenotherapy? Yes and no.

Adler often spoke of patients who shortly before the successful termination of a long treatment arranged new difficulties. They wanted to be cured, but they did not want the therapist to take the credit. One is reminded of Napoleon, who indeed asked the Pope to participate in his coronation, but only up to the critical moment, when the actual ceremony was to be consummated; then he took the crown from the Pope's hands and placed it on his own head. He did not want to be indebted to anyone but himself. There are likewise patients who "reward" the therapist for his successful efforts by feigning failure at the last moment. Anyone who knows the neurotic's huge propensity for trying to cover the shortest distance by the most roundabout path will realize how problematic any comparative critique of the results of psychotherapeutic treatment becomes, especially when the critique is undertaken largely by experimental psychologists, especially behaviorists. In all fairness I must add that Hans Eysenck includes in his summary many studies by psychotherapists, usually psychoanalysts, who came to similar conclusions. This can be explained by the fact that they use the same methods for their investigations as the behaviorists and experimental psychologists. These methods may be quite precise and well suited to measuring many things, but of course they are hardly adequate for something that defies measurement and often cannot be expressed in statistics.

Although Eysenck's work should be taken seriously, the fact remains that he hardly touches upon the really momentous problems that must be dealt with before one can properly discuss the overall issue of psychology's effectiveness, which, after all, is his topic. I have gone to considerable lengths to show that all psychic manifestations remain incomprehensible if one fails to examine them in their

indissoluble relatedness or if within that context one ig-
nores the central issue, namely, the relation of the individual
to himself, to others, to the world. From these factors one
can attempt to reconstruct a person's reference system.
Merely sending a child to a kindergarten produces a complex net of relationships, references and reactions. How
complex then must be the web that connects the psychotherapist and his patient! Everything has psychic reverber-
ations, thanks to the patient's reference system, his relationship to all his experiences, to people and to the therapist's techniques. Thus it becomes possible for the patient
to be seduced by the echo of his own voice or by that of
another voice which he himself dreams up and endows
with speech.

For some time now psychotherapists, and especially
orthodox psychoanalysts, have refused to accept any patient
until they are sure that his neurosis does not have some
peculiarity or particular trait which will make him unsuited for their method of treatment. An experienced therapist can easily determine within the space of a one-hour
conversation whether he would succeed in establishing
that cooperative relationship essential to any therapeutic
treatment. Here, too, the personal relationship is more
important than most of the other factors one must consider if one wants to arrive at a fair assessment of psychotherapy.

But the problem could be formulated the other way
around: perhaps these other factors are precisely what
determines whether or not the desired relationship can be
created. From a methodological standpoint this angle of
inquiry would doubtless be more justified. However, examination of these factors properly belongs to the treat-

ment, and what one may expect of the treatment will be determined at least negatively the moment the therapist and his patient first meet. Therefore an examination of the effectiveness of psychotherapy can only proceed after those cases have been eliminated in which treatment began under unfavorable circumstances, the most unfavorable being the recognizable impossibility of establishing a fruitful working relationship between patient and doctor. A corollary would be that a certain therapist may be bad for one patient but excellent for another. Yet it may be even more crucial that only a relatively small percentage of medically and nonmedically trained psychotherapists have the requisite character, intuition and grasp of human nature to treat the emotionally disturbed.

In this connection we agree with Paul Meehl, former president of the American Psychological Association, who surveyed psychotherapists on the question of their colleagues' competency; he discovered that "less than half, actually closer to one-third or one-fourth of local practitioners" were thought by their colleagues to be worth recommending. That means that more than sixty per cent of those practicing were held to be beneath the standard for the profession. The same psychologist shares the view of Hans Eysenck that no study has yet shown clear proof that "uncovering, insight-facilitating, interpretive, analytically oriented" psychotherapy represents a really effective means of cure.[2]

Is the systematic training dispensed by the various schools of psychotherapy calculated to improve the character and therapeutic abilities of the would-be therapists, the analyst-analysands, as they might be called? One is reminded of the character in a famous French comedy who beats his breast and proclaims, "That is my opinion, and personally,

I share it." The first prerequisite in psychoanalytic training is that the trainees accept the orthodox doctrines of their various sects as irrefutable; they must share them so fully that no room is left for other opinions or even a whisper of doubt.

What happens to these future psychotherapists is the same thing that happens to most of their patients, who in the course of prolonged treatment come to appropriate the analysts' ideas and finally turn them into self-fulfilling prophecies. In their "free" associations and dreams, in genuine or less genuine recollections, they more and more tend to come forth with precisely the information that fits the analysts' theories. In the end, the result is exactly what Karl Kraus formulated as a definition of psychoanalysis: "Pyschoanalysis is the mental illness for whose therapy it mistakes itself." At the time this definition seemed grotesquely unfair, and it still does, but there is something to it. For psychoanalytic interpretation may provide many patients with the ingredients of a neurosis with which they can replace the apparently cured disorder that caused them to seek help in the first place. Confusion begins to take over. An echo is taken for an answering voice. The patient tailors his dreams more and more to the interpretations he has become used to and produces psychotherapeutically prefabricated symbols. The therapist believes the dreams to be authentic, for that is his opinion and he shares it. He is sure that he has no preconceptions, but since he already has an end-result in mind, he only draws out of the patient what he or his theory has already stuffed into him. The danger of this kind of self-deception really should have been recognized quite early; its first victim was none other than Sigmund Freud himself.

For four years, until the autumn of 1897, Freud was caught in the meshes of this self-fulfilling method. He managed to obtain the same startling admission from each of his hysteria patients: each one had been molested sexually in her childhood by her father—*voilà!* Freud decided that this traumatic experience was the decisive cause of hysteria. On May 2, 1896 he read a paper before the Vienna Society for Psychiatry and Neurology on the eighteen cases he had analyzed thoroughly. Without exception they lent support to his theory of molestation. Freud went so far as to declare unabashedly before the group of largely disapproving experts that he had found the source of the Nile in neuropathology. One and one-half years later, on September 21, 1897, he wrote his friend Wilhelm Fliess in Berlin:

. . . I will confide in you at once the great secret that has been slowly dawning on me in the last months. I no longer believe in my *neurotica*. . . . (Thus, the possibility remained open that sexual phantasy invariably seizes upon the theme of the parents.) . . . I have no idea now where I have got to, since I have not achieved a theoretical understanding of repression and its interplay of forces. It seems to have become once again arguable that it is only later experiences that give the impetus to phantasies, which then hark back to childhood. . . .[3]

One need not draw conclusions from this episode as to the path Freud took next; it led back to the original fiction, which he now merely reversed: from this time on it was no longer the fathers who molested their daughters, but the children who wanted to sleep with one parent and exterminate the other! The Nile had dried up, but its source had remained. I cite this remarkable and extremely revealing case because it shows that the tyranny of the echo began to manifest itself when interpretive psycho-therapy was in its earliest stages.

But aside from the risk of inducing the patient to con-firm a false diagnosis or interpretation, offered in good faith, of course, there are much greater risks, risks that no school of therapy has yet dealt with adequately and which possibly can never be avoided.

When the neurotic voluntarily or under pressure from his family and friends seeks treatment, it is because he is struggling in vain with difficulties that he cannot cir-cumvent except by neurotic arrangements, which in turn make each passing day more unbearable, for they intensify his conflict with the outside world. No matter what method the therapist employs, he has to begin the treat-ment by providing the patient with a "temporary dis-charge": the patient is told he may, and in fact should, retreat from the front lines, since in his present condition he is in no position to grapple with his problems, let alone solve them. He should therefore stop torturing himself with them. Therapy gives him a furlough; it begins by indulging him, returning to or continuing the pampering the patient once received from his immediate environment. That pampering had become ineffective when the individual was forced to confront adult problems and solve them on his own. This sort of confrontation makes many people orphans long before the death of their parents.

The therapist's first move offers a new kind of pamper-ing, perhaps on a higher plane than the family's, which can be assumed to have already failed. To use another meta-phor: the doctor gives the schoolboy shaken by exam-time panic the right to withdraw from the examination without any particularly sound reasons or pretexts such as an upset stomach, a mysterious fever, sleeplessness or a legitimate illness. The therapist allows a similar retreat in the face of difficult decisions: getting engaged or married, applying for a divorce, accepting or leaving a job, and so forth. This absence from the scene of struggle during the first phase of treatment is one of the most important reasons for the patient's attempting to maneuver the therapist into a mother- or father-position and behaving like a helpless, sometimes intractable child badly in need of love. This would seem to be a very strong inducement for the psychoanalyst to view the release of the libido and its transference from the parents to the therapist as an absolutely necessary step. He will bring about the transference intentionally if it does not take place by itself. Later on, when the patient is supposed to leave his refuge and think and behave independently, the transference becomes a handicap. Sometimes it lingers on and ruins a lengthy course of treatment. Freud interprets this special relationship that springs up in the first phase of therapy as a transference; it can also be viewed as the recreation of a relationship that gives the neurotic necessary protection against the demands of reality; he shows his gratitude by being willing to open up somewhat. No matter which interpretation we choose, we know that at this stage the patient feels he has won a victory. That is why he immediately begins to treat the therapist. I say "treat" because in fact the therapist often falls into the patient's trap, especially if he believes in the value of transference and has worked a little too hard at establishing it. Then he will find it difficult to undo the reversal of roles; the patient remains a prisoner because he does not want to release his guard. From this moment on the therapist is merely a prisoner of his prisoner.

In the second phase the doctor sets about expanding the

patient's consciousness, and now the resistance present from the outset breaks forth in a variety of forms. The patient wants to keep his initial advantage, but he does not want to accept any changes. Here and there he makes tiny concessions, modifies a symptom or relinquishes it entirely. Thus begins the struggle with the angel; its outcome will determine the success or failure of the treatment. And here we must again take up questions we have already dealt with at length, specifically those which have a bearing on consciousness and the unconscious.

In connection with Freud's strange experience and his rape-fiction, which finally turned out to be psychic rape by the therapist, one finds in the letter quoted above both a courageous acknowledgment of error and the following statement:

If in this way we see that the unconscious never overcomes the resistance of the conscious, then, too, we lose our expectation that in treatment the opposite will happen, to the extent of the unconscious being completely tamed by the conscious.[4]

That is an extraordinarily important doubt. Unfortunately Freud did not harbor it for long. Shortly thereafter he achieved other certainties: he thought he had found a second source of the Nile. But in his letter of September 1897, in which he does not yet speak of the subconscious, he is pondering with his usual shrewdness the difficulty, indeed the impossibility, of creating full awareness. He begins to see how fluid the actual boundary is between conscious and unconscious; he also sees that that boundary can sometimes become an impregnable barrier. I have already suggested that as far as this problem is concerned one can only hope to find a more or less convincing explanation, useful for educational or therapeutic purposes, but not definitive.

Every individual uses things that have happened to him as raw material for the production of his guiding principle. Often he totally changes the actual implications of these events. These manipulated events he mistakenly equates with experience and fashions his schema of apperception from them. This in turn helps his conscious mind register only that which suits its purposes, i.e., that which confirms his original assessments and prevents doubts from arising. The therapist is like the rest of humanity: he perceives and experiences according to a schema of apperception. Consequently, he interprets his patients' experiences according to his own principle of selection and treats his patients according to his own guiding principle as a psychologist, as a therapist, and as an individual. We have already established that therapy is a relationship: it is an encounter between two characters, two modes of apperception and two equally determined and determining consciousnesses. The extent of the therapist's subjectivity is lessened to a degree by the fact that he adheres to the theories and techniques of a certain school, but this does not alter the basic situation. With time the patient transforms himself into the parrot of his therapist, who may himself be someone else's parrot. Yet each of them basically remains faithful to his own leitmotif.

When it comes to weighing the relative success or failure of psychotherapeutic methods, another more important scruple arises. The most telling objection one could —and perhaps should—raise concerns the almost unavoidable misuse by the neurotic of the insights offered him by therapy.

Regardless of whether he is treated by a Freudian, a Jungian or some other analyst, or by an individual psychologist, the patient learns from his therapist that his disorders are connected with his early childhood, with his upbringing, with his parents, his siblings and many things for which he bears no responsibility. Individual psychology does not credit experiences with autonomous significance and considers the influence of traumas to be only relatively unimportant, sometimes even negligible. Nevertheless the first thing the patient learns in individual psychology is that he is a victim. He is not to blame for his failures, his cowardice, his evasions, his tendency to disparage himself, his striving for unearned recognition and superiority, his longing to receive love without offering anything in return, or his tyrannical jealousy. Nor is he responsible for his fearfulness, his anxiety, and the various manipulations and arrangements with which he tries to avoid the demands of life while demanding the utmost of life for himself. He is a victim and can do nothing about it— and all because of the helpless state in which he came into the world, because his father did such-and-such, his mother did thus-and-so, and his sister or his brother or both did so-and-so. Because, because, because . . . In short, everything would have been different if only he had not . . . Latin has the perfect word for these people: *nisi*—"If . . . not." They should be called "nisi-ites." "Nisi" should be the only inscription on the heroic monument they think they deserve. For what might they not have accomplished if . . . and if things had not . . . !

As we stated, psychotherapy begins by giving the patient a temporary discharge. The neurotic all too often evaluates the knowledge thus imparted to him and refashions it so that he can use it as a weapon against his parents, living or dead, against his sisters and brothers, against his closest friends, against his sweetheart, his wife, his own children, against his colleagues and collaborators, against his superiors and his subordinates, against everyone but himself—except when he reproaches himself pro forma without any serious intention of reforming.

People go through life brandishing extremely satisfying grudges against their fathers and mothers, against the Oedipus complex; more and more autobiographies nowadays attest that this complex has made emotional cripples of their authors for life. Others rely on their inferiority feelings to obtain sympathy, or on their discouragement, which prevents them from carrying out the three tasks Adler terms essential. Depending on which school their therapists belong to, they complain about the tyranny of the id or the ego or the excessive demands of the superego, about their own or someone else's lack of social feeling, about traumatic experiences which, now that they are aware of them, they can neither pardon nor forget, and above all about the fact that the people with whom they have to live are terribly neurotic and show absolutely no sympathy or understanding.

Hans Eysenck's observation that one could obtain the same success with other methods as with psychotherapy did not actually challenge therapy's effectiveness—and properly so, for there is no doubt that therapy can quickly eliminate or reduce to an acceptable minimum most symptoms of neurosis, particularly nervous disorders of various organs. The same is true of certain anxiety states and anxieties. In the case of Mrs. C., for example, such striking results were achieved after a few sessions that the patient considered herself cured; she was able to go outdoors unaccompanied. After a few weeks or months she even forgot that this had ever presented a problem. If given a reasonable amount of time, therapy can also help the patient to solve his current conflicts; it gives him insight into their nature and the necessary courage to set about his tasks without further procrastination.

A therapist of any school will always try to get his patient to admit that some problems will never be solved to his complete satisfaction and that he should not postpone decisions too long in his search for the "absolutely right" one; he has already delayed too much. The good therapist tries to instill in his patient the courage to remain imperfect. The therapist wants to awaken in the patient a sense for the universal logic of life and a realization that an unswerving application of his own private logic will eventually prove his undoing. Certain doctors, convinced that they should not give advice, may adhere strictly to the principle of nonintervention, since full consciousness will be sufficient to liberate the patient from his current conflicts as well as from the whole burden of his past. Even so, these therapists cannot help exercising an educative function. In fact, no person who comes in close contact with another person can avoid exercising this function—for better or for worse.

The seemingly neutral analyst long ago gave in and accepted the logic of human life formulated most clearly by Adler; he now recognizes the necessity of practicing the so-called ego therapy for which psychoanalysts once arrogantly mocked individual psychologists. Adler explained:

To cure a neurosis and a psychosis it is necessary to change completely the whole up-bringing of the patient and turn him definitely and unconditionally back upon human society.[5]

But how does one reeducate a person? How does one correct mistakes that have grown out of a way of life, and how does one enable the runaway to return to the community? By enlarging his consciousness?

In spite of the doubt cast nowadays on the theory of the conscious and the unconscious by the popular theory of conditioning and by behaviorism, the fact remains that one cannot overcome one's past without a fundamental increase in awareness. Bringing-to-consciousness succeeds only when it includes a reexperiencing and reevaluating of past events. We attempt to revive a phase of the past which long ago lost its immediacy. We try to make it part of the present, but in a limited sense. The next step entails rediscovery, valuable only if it also means revision. Someone who can remember in this fashion confronts the past as both long-lost experience fetched out of the depths of the memory, and as newly understood experience. New insight merges with the recollection of the event to produce a dramatically revised experience.

We are objects of our past, victims not so much of what actually happened as of what we made of it through misunderstanding and misinterpretation. By actively dominating the past, one liberates oneself from it and transforms it into an objective image of something that once existed and never will again.

Perhaps we should not speak of liberation from the past as if it were possible and had already been achieved by someone somewhere. No one can free himself from his past without destroying part of himself, a part not entirely necessary but certainly irreplaceable. Therapy does not aim at this destructive sort of liberation, but at the unique and revolutionary experience of reliving and revising one's past. Hegel's word *aufheben* would fit here; it unites the concepts of eliminating and preserving which are characteristic of the therapeutic process. One extracts and files away everything that henceforth is to remain inoperative, past and gone—for example, prohibitions and obligations that have become meaningless in the course of time. The positive side of the same term suggests that one saves that which is worth saving.

Thus we return to the problem of choice. We all choose at some point the identity we would like to have and exclude anything that would interfere. But this choice, which is made according to a criterion we apply with total or partial awareness, will determine every future decision on alternatives. In the beginning the possibilities are practically if not mathematically infinite. Countless doors stand open before us. Every time we pass through a door, the number of doors available decreases. The choices are still there behind us, but we can never turn back. Thus with every step we sacrifice countless possibilities, perhaps choosing the very one that we should have avoided. The present swallows more potential future than anyone could hope to experience.

Thus our selection of the first door is all-important. How do we decide on our criterion, which we later apply as if it were the only one we could conceive of? The whole thing becomes a vicious circle: we are prisoners of our own premises, which seize hold of us before we have time to test them and reject them if necessary.

Unless therapy manages to change a patient's schema of apperception, it can produce at best superficial improvement, although that may give a certain satisfaction. Everything in Eysenck's investigation revolves around this kind of improvement, whether he depicts it as such or as a definite cure. But the difference is fundamental, for the success we are speaking of (it should not even be called a cure) is in reality the result of self-education, of reeducation and additional education. As unbelievable as it may sound, success means creating the desire and the capacity to start afresh. This desire cannot happen, however, without massive encouragement, i.e., without liberation from the inferiority feelings which have accompanied the patient since early childhood. The encouragement combines the two forms of psychological activity: on the one hand, insight and understanding are achieved through application of scientifically verifiable methods of argumentation, and on the other, an artistic process is set in motion, a process similar to that achieved by particularly gifted educators. What do we mean here by artistic? Many things, but surely the art of dealing with human beings must be part of it. By means of this encouragement the therapist succeeds in bringing the patient to the point at which he can and wants to risk going over his past. Every successful foray strengthens him in his choice of a new path and makes further advances easier. But he can continue only if his consciousness expands and he sees the biases that limit his apperception; he must realize how confining his way of viewing things is. At such moments the contradiction becomes so dramatic that a revolutionary solution is called for. The patient catches himself *in flagranti*, his eyes are opened, and he suddenly understands that he has been going around with blinders on. But how can he perceive his own schema of apperception if that is the filter through which he sees the world? The example that illustrates how this becomes possible is borrowed from the realm of religious experience:

Many a person of high intelligence—a man, for instance, like Blaise Pascal—has experienced sudden illumination. The effect is as if he saw for the first time the landscape in which he has spent his entire life. Only now does he notice the glowing light that has burned before his eyes since childhood. Suddenly he receives a message; he has known every word of it for a long, long time, known it but not decoded it or not read it, or if read, not understood it, or if understood not acknowledged it. After this revelation he leaves the shelter in which he has hitherto found protection, but only to give himself over into the protection of the Almighty.

One can expect nothing of this kind in psychology; there inspiration would be more suspect than welcome. Examples from religious experience abound, but are applicable in psychology only insofar as we seem in both cases to be dealing with a sudden change in vision. One sees things differently from before, one sees different things, and much of what remains the same appears in a light which changes to reveal a meaning different from the one we had taken for granted.

One patient had been accustomed from childhood on to approach others with his hand outstretched to receive gifts: "What do you have for me?" He became more and more disgruntled as people began to fail him and finally stopped giving altogether when they realized that he never gave anything in return. All those he had contact with became prisoners of his schema of apperception; they ceased to exist as soon as they went out of his life. If he found them in a bad mood he assumed that they were angry with him and harbored a secret resentment against him; he found this exceedingly unfair. If they were in a good mood he thought they wanted to show how indifferent they were to him and his troubles.

This type of egocentric individual finally comes to a

dead end; he no longer understands the world. How can one make him realize that others have a right to an autonomous existence, that they need not depend on him, the neurotic? How can one make him realize that he will mean less and less to others if he continues to demand without giving, if he remains a person no one can rely upon? The moment this psychological beggar comes to recognize the existence of others not only as independent but as equal, his manner of vision will change, his eyes open; he will find that in fact he must learn to see anew; he must *learn*.

Adler recognized this necessity very early, several decades before those who invented the conditioning or behavioral therapy so admired by Eysenck and others like him. According to individual psychology, it is not sufficient for the patient to recognize why he has always opposed himself, why he has always placed stumbling blocks between himself and the longed-for goal. His insight will not be complete until he has learned how to behave appropriately. He must master the art of taking large and small steps; he must experience in daily behavioral training how one becomes a fellow man, how one changes from a receiver to a mutualist, a giver-receiver. Adler taught that this training in constant self-education must begin during therapy; for bringing-to-consciousness will not succeed unless the patient is being trained for life at the same time. The success of his self-training will help him move in the direction of conscious experience. It is not enough to have been born a human being; one must learn to live as a fellow man.

Chapter VIII

C AN ONE TEACH ANYTHING, learn anything? No, not anything, but a good deal—almost everything that a human being can transmit or offer to another: manual and
mental techniques, human interaction, and in particular
love. But there remains when all is said and done an unsolved problem—Adler called it the *"Pest problem,"* the
residual problem; one becomes painfully aware of it in
certain situations, as if it signified total failure. Sometimes,
as with an incurable illness, the only refuge seems to be
death. At such times one tends to feel, think and behave as
if everything depended on this last unsolved problem, as
if one could never be happy without finding the solution.
Our over-sensitivity in this regard stems from our striving
for perfection, our yearning for a godlike absolute. This
yearning is an important component in all lust for power.
A person who cannot find the courage to be imperfect will
pine away from dissatisfaction, and his gaze will remain
fixed on what has apparently been granted to others but
denied to him.

Learning, or life-training as a method, is the most effective means of adaptation. Once we are no longer inclined

to or able to learn, psychic old age sets in. This is all the more serious since most human beings lost this inclination and capacity relatively early. The process of aging begins long before the calendar suggests it. Adler's studies on neurosis show that the neurotic frequently shirks the task of learning in childhood and therefore acts only according to stereotypes.

This phenomenon is important not only for psychopathology but for any understanding of human nature, for it allows us to examine the vital matter of adaptation from another angle and helps us formulate a precise definition of the limitations imposed on each individual's and each generation's adaptability. In terms of both individual and social psychology, no man belongs only to his own time or chronological generation. A good part of him belongs to the generation of his parents, and this remains the case throughout his life. The overlapping of generations makes itself felt in everyone's life and is as unavoidable as his parasitic beginnings. He becomes part of his own generation, but the integration process stops all too soon. Around the age of thirty, if not sooner, many change from active participants into silent bystanders; they have found their niche, have a family and a roof over their heads, and their every move has long since become automatic. From now on their gait takes on its firmness not from youthful vigor and courage but from the confidence that comes of inflexible routine. Since they always take the same path, their consciousness does not even need to be activated; their feet already know the terrain.

Human beings lack natural instincts, and without mechanical aids life would be impossible. This automatic functioning is indispensable for performing everyday tasks as well as complicated intellectual work. The number of automatic routines available to us is ever on the increase in modern technological society, with its far-reaching automation of production and distribution. But what distinguishes the stereotypes of neurotic behavior with their equally automated small catastrophes and melodramatic threats from the socially useful automation without which daily life would be unthinkable?

Here we encounter one of those fundamental problems that each individual experiences as something totally unique, although it concerns all mankind. The basic issue here is the contradiction that we cannot become what we are without being dominated by what we have learned: often we *must* do what we *can* do simply because we can do it. With every new series of actions we can perform without activating our conscious attention, we voluntarily and usually gladly relinquish a portion of our freedom. If we wish to modify or relinquish an automatic reaction, we must shatter it like a mold. For along with the freedom we gain from automatic functioning, we constantly risk being transformed into machines that produce old junk. We cannot manage without automatisms to take care of tedious and repetitive tasks, but we sink far below our proper level if we fail to constantly question their usefulness. While adapting to the everyday necessities, we must try to keep as much freedom as possible, freedom to grow and to respond to new situations and experiences.

Since we stop developing at an early age, we pass up untold opportunities and allow much of our potential to wither on the vine. Man is surely the most wasteful creature whom absurdly wasteful nature has yet produced—wasteful of himself. We make do with about one-tenth of our potential and leave the other nine-tenths to molder like the contents of a warehouse we have either never discovered or else totally forgotten. Thus we neglect the greatest possibilities afforded by our freedom, the freedom which would make self-renewal conceivable and would enable us to question ourselves constantly without losing our equilibrium in the process.

There is a saying Marx attributes to Hegel concerning repetition of certain events: the first time an event occurs it is tragic, but when repeated it becomes a farce, a parody of itself. Although this is a saying, not an established truth, it does appear that man himself has a hand in what appears as tragic destiny: either one decides that repetitious tragic experiences are the ineluctable work of fate, or one sees through them and rewrites the tragedy as a comedy. Once he realizes this he can be more objective toward himself and can view his past as just one of many possible variations not at all as inevitable. Everything might have turned out differently. In this light fate reveals itself as a pretext, a crutch for the "nisi-ites."

Reexperiencing the past contributes greatly to self-liberation, providing it involves not merely a rediscovery of the past, but also a critique of the present—a critique which helps us to overcome the present. This *fruitful* kind of repetition is rare, however. In point of fact, to form psychological automatic functionings one must repeat over and over again those gestures that offer the best possible adjustment to situations and tasks one knows will remain essentially the same over a long period of time. For example: a person who climbs the same set of stairs every night in total darkness will soon be able to do so with the same sure-footedness he would display in broad daylight. He will be able to trust his feet to adjust automatically to the familiar irregularities. If he comes home one night completely sober and stumbles, then slips and falls, he will think that something has gone awry with him, that some unconscious psychic factor has interfered with his well-established automatic function. He may then wonder how to interpret this malfunction, trying to discover the unconscious motivation for his accident. But the next day he must relinquish his suspicion when he finds that the step he tripped on was broken. The step was in the wrong, not his automated feet.

We cannot live without adapting in various ways to quite a number of unchanging conditions. Automatic functioning is essential to life, but it can change into disruptive, dangerous obstructions, a threat to community life, if we cling to it after the conditions calling it forth have changed.

Since life involves constant motion and change, adaptation must obviously be more than merely passive. If an individual adapts to circumstances, conditions, relationships, prohibitions and duties without adapting these things to himself as well, he will start out with such limitations that he will always lead the existence of a moron, caught up in endless stereotype repetition. He will remain an object, a plaything of fate. He will fear fate like the devil yet worship it like a god. If human beings were capable only of passive adaptation, we would still be sitting in the trees, Adler used to say.

One thing is certain in the history of mankind: it is a history of the active adaptation whereby man adjusts conditions to himself, changing them as far as possible to fit his own goals. Man usually does this so successfully that subsequent generations find themselves confronted by totally different conditions, which they in turn modify. One can regard all human activity as the dialectical give-and-take between active and passive adaptation; this dialectic reflects a basic truth about our lives: we cannot be all subject or all object, although we often perceive ourselves as only one or the other.

In the first phase of life, learning is an activity, but, to paraphrase Nietzsche, one essentially like that of the camel allowing itself to be loaded. One takes things in, passively, unquestioningly. But if information taken in is not processed and digested in a second phase, it will soon lose immediacy and be eliminated for good. This happens with much of what children learn in school when preparing for tests. The example of learning a foreign language is very apt: even if one learned all the words in the dictionary, one would still be unable to carry on a conversation in the new tongue unless one had also learned to activate the words, to transform them into thoughts. One must master the language, not merely be laden down with its vocabulary like a camel.

When a person performs any act, he usually steps outside himself and moves toward something; he seizes hold of it. Many believe that man cannot live without repeated acts of aggression. He demolishes food—this begins soon after his birth—and he behaves aggressively toward the first things he can lay hands on. Touching, grabbing, hitting and discarding these objects is a necessary part of learning. But does that mean, as we are often told today, that all our misfortunes are traceable to human aggression, and that the total destruction of the human race is inevitable unless we can learn to curb our aggressive urges?

Among modern psychologists, Alfred Adler was the first to point out aggression as a general and characteristic phenomenon; he attributed much greater importance to it than did Freud, who considered the libido primary. In 1908 Adler delivered a lecture before the Congress of Psychoanalysts in Salzburg entitled "The Aggression Drive in Life and in Neurosis." Adler later abandoned psychology of drives and the jargon that went with it, instead applying the methods of individual psychology to those phenomena he had traced back to the aggressive instinct; he studied them in the context of the human being as a consistent whole.

Is aggression really a general characteristic of human beings, as we hear more and more often nowadays? Before I address myself to this question I must remind the reader that the sciences and scholarly disciplines are as prone as haute couture to fads and fashions. An example of faddishness in the intellectual world is the recent tendency to explain man by his similarity to the animals. This fashion recurs two or three times a century.

It is difficult enough to fathom human consciousness, even given man's ability to express abstractions in words. To seek an understanding of human nature in the behavior of animals is a curious folly. It gives pleasure to the sort of person who likes to see an ape wearing a tie and smoking a cigar or a trained dog standing on his hind legs and barking into a telephone. Thus attempts have been made to find the basis of human aggression by relating it to observations and anthropomorphizing interpretations of animal behavior. Of course zoological research is valuable, as is our experience with domestic animals, but most of what is said about the emotional life of animals indicates more about the person who says it than about zoological facts.

But let us return to the question of aggression, which arises as soon as a psychologist observes a young infant. The first tensions a child experiences are absolutely intolerable, usually a source of boundless despair. But as soon as the child discovers that something always happens to allay his distress, he tries to force adults to come to his aid as fast as possible. But even the most obtuse nanny or the most inexperienced mother can recognize the screaming that betokens a bad mood, the screaming that expresses extreme tension, and the other signals that the child sends out to his immediate environment, the *socially addressed* signals. We know that children discover quite early that they can secure the availability and pleasant company of a person by sending out these emergency signals, even when no tension exists to justify them. If one examines good photographs of children screaming for this purpose, their faces reveal clear aggression.

On this lowest level of aggression as well as on the highest, one always finds that the starting point is a rapid increase of tension, a sense of dissatisfaction, even of great need, and in extreme cases the fear of being overwhelmed by a superior force; sometimes pain takes on this aspect. On a somewhat higher level than the infant's, hunger, pain or some other physical discomfort can mix with anxiety to produce and at the same time mask aggression. This anxiety functions as a cry for help; in my book on tyranny I called this "socially addressed anxiety." Every human being is acquainted with it, for we have all suffered from and utilized it in early childhood, and to the end of our days we remain capable of summoning it up and even enjoying it. The child who starts out of his sleep screaming with nocturnal terror and forces his parents to shower him with solicitude and tenderness is undoubtedly committing an act of aggression, but in a manner which allows him to feel that he alone is the victim. This behavior is so characteristic that one may make two fundamental observations:

1. Aggression born of feelings of insecurity and inferiority and expressed as socially addressed anxiety manifests

itself in those who are confident that their call will bring help and that their aggression will be effective, thanks to the compliance of those around them.

2. Aggression of this kind is usually directed toward those whom a person, justifiedly or unjustifiedly, feels sure of. It therefore starts out as a means of protecting or extending threatened privileges or preferential treatment within one's own circle. This aggression represents an easy way of obtaining love and tenderness within the family. Here aggressiveness is disguised as a noble form of weakness. But the revealing switch to really injurious assault can take place in a moment. The goal is not self-assertion but gaining superiority over all those who are to be exploited, as well as over actual or presumed rivals. In children and adolescents one often encounters the typical form of aggression that authoritarian adults call impudence; it first appears within the family and tacitly demands understanding, good will and tolerance on the part of those very people against whom it is directed. No one can be so easily and thoroughly intimidated as a little brat who is suddenly refused sympathy.

One can likewise observe that aggressive children who seem to rule effortlessly over everyone in the family will withdraw into the darkest corner and become incapable of standing up for themselves once their tried-and-true method is thwarted by outsiders who refuse to play along. These children then resort to tantrums or sulking.

But let us examine a typical example of socially addressed and concealed aggression. Mr. D., a man of fifty, holds a rather high position in a bank. Due to his competence and his extremely pleasant demeanor, he is much esteemed by his superiors. He is friendly toward his subordinates, although he insists somewhat pedantically that everything be done exactly according to his instructions. His acquaintances know him as a faithful husband and a good father to his four children. It is thought that this man leads a happy family life: everything functions as well in his home as in his office.

But on closer inspection one discovers that his relationship to his wife, his children, his relatives and close friends is based on rules which he alone has set up; and if they are not observed he suffers from poor health and depression. In his youth D. had an operation; this operation is mentioned again and again as if it had been very grave and not without after-effects. Actually the operation merely involved removal of an inflamed appendix. D. had proclaimed a sort of postoperative state of emergency, shrouded in secrecy. The life of the family is molded by the considerateness D. demands. Anyone who comes to the house learns that there is something special about D.'s health, something which he bears heroically but which requires that he be extremely careful. He is not supposed to smoke, but he does so with great gusto after a good meal, while waiting for the members of his family to beg him to stop after a few puffs lest he endanger his health. He usually gives in with a loud sigh. If this request should not be forthcoming, D. feels neglected and hurt. Soon everyone notices that he is not feeling well. Accompanied by his wife and children he withdraws, and the evening comes to an abrupt end. D. likes to talk about himself and his delicate condition, but he wants to be urged. He likes to appear to be dispensing favors; when actually it is he who is on the receiving end.

What is aggressive about this behavior? Ostensibly nothing. That his almost grown-up children have to be home at an early hour because their worried father will not be able to go to sleep otherwise—is that an aggressive demand? Yes, it is. It takes the form of socially addressed anxiety and exorbitant expectations. In childhood D. often contracted a temporary fever or some other symptom if his younger sister brought home a better report card than his. Of course he was immediately fussed over, with the result that his sister's achievements were forgotten. D. is by no means authoritarian; on the contrary, he is gentle and good-natured, but he has retained this style of reacting since childhood.

As a child he was often overcome, especially on the way home from school, by a sudden terrible suspicion that his parents were ill or had died. His parents were touched by his concern and decided to devote more time to him than to the other children, in order to reassure him by their presence. For a time he was fetched from school alternately by his mother and father. Was D. aggressive? His parents would have denied it. We have the greatest difficulty and resistance to seeing through those deceptive manifestations that are calculated to flatter us or answer our secret wishes.

Since the number of people who were neglected or short-changed in childhood by those around them is relatively small, most of us have had a more or less pampered childhood, and socially addressed aggressiveness is the most widespread form of aggression. However, there is a more threatening form, which represents compensation for aggressive anxiety and is closely related to the inferiority complex. Just as the inferiority complex is neurotic compensation for feelings of inferiority, *totalitarian aggressiveness* is compensation for aggressive anxiety. We can also note another similarity: socially addressed aggressiveness expresses itself in exaggerated flattery, obsequiousness, marked expressions of tenderness, in extreme solicitude for parents and friends. It helps create a desire for recognition and intensifies this desire into a striving for superiority. Here we have the effort I alluded to earlier to achieve a central position within the community, since the community is to provide recognition and tender admiration. And recognition is gladly granted to an individual who expresses admiration; he is recognized in order that the recognition he offers in return may be all the more highly valued!

Aggressive anxiety is one of the most important causes of the desire for power and at the same time its best concealed characteristic. Since equality with his fellow men is intolerable to the power-hungry person, he must employ every means to prove their inferiority, that is, he must produce situations in which they will find themselves inferior to him or at least give the appearance that this is the case. The individual suffering from aggressive anxiety strives for total power, for he fears, though he does not think it consciously, that incomplete power is tantamount to powerlessness. A person will admit to harboring socially addressed anxiety, although not the corresponding aggressiveness; but a victim of aggressive anxiety will not acknowledge his problem to himself any more than the power-hungry individual will admit to his insecurity. For this reason aggressive anxiety always manifests itself as totalitarian aggression. Let me repeat a metaphorical example that I employed, and not by chance, in my analysis of tyranny:

E., the leader of a totalitarian party, suffers from aggressive anxiety. Now he has to pass through a forest by night. Too cowardly to confess that he is afraid, he manages to convince his companions that this forest is bristling with enemy troops and assassins waiting for him. He creates a plan which has to be carried out to the letter: the forest has to be set on fire and fired upon with all available weapons.

Naturally E. takes the command and moves with his bodyguard to a safe position. Later our hero advances fearlessly into the charred forest with his heavily armed troops. . . . More elaborate and characteristic details could be added if this were more than an ad hoc example that I used in 1937, with two contemporaries in mind, men who had millions of followers—Adolf Hitler and Stalin.

If social conditions are favorable, aggressive anxiety often pushes its victims into the political arena, where their total aggressiveness finds justification in a totalitarian ideology and triumphs with the victory of that ideology.

Apart from these two forms of neurotic aggression, there is everyday *competitive aggressiveness*, to be found in the rivalry one encounters in all societies and every social situation. One finds it in kindergartens and among the feeble inmates of old people's homes, as well as among people in the prime of life. This aggressiveness represents primarily a historically and socially much modified and modifiable form of the struggle for existence, but it also reflects the attempt of every individual to justify his own existence by acquiring a sense of his own worth that is corroborated by others; everyone strives to gain recognition for his person in all its uniqueness.

Without food one starves, and without self-esteem one perishes; one loses oneself and every reason for living. Only a person who is sure of his value can prevent the natural and necessary desire to compare himself with others from degenerating into a compulsion; only a man who feels sufficiently recognized by his loved ones can forego pursuing self-aggrandizement in every situation and resist the temptation to diminish others—"the deprecation tendency," as Adler called it. This most widespread form of human aggression repeatedly disrupts human relations, but it never destroys them, for everyday compromises restore the general equilibrium. No one escapes this aggressiveness, for no one but idiots and psychotics fully succeeds in preserving the certainty of his own value. It is threatened on all sides: in the family, in school, in one's profession, in marriage, in all relationships.

In addition, a general hunger for recognition exists. It would be absurd to call it a product of modern society, which in fact possesses practically unlimited means for distributing recognition as it sees fit, as well as for increasing personal and social desire for recognition to fever pitch. The desire for recognition has existed in every society, in inaccessible mountain villages or in the crowded slums of ancient Rome, in every shop, in every guild, within all families and estates. To be sure, the forms of the struggle for existence and the struggle for self-esteem have changed with changing social conditions, but they have always exercised an immense influence on life in society. Perhaps some socialist society might succeed in abolishing material necessity and poverty and would thereby actually put an end to the struggle for existence. But no society of any kind could so change human beings that they could bear to be rejected as worthless or contemptible. No one can maintain self-esteem all by himself, even if he lives in a special solitude.

There have doubtless been times in which human beings were far more aggressive than they are today, readier to resort to violence, either because they despaired of securing their rights by any other means or because the threat of violence constituted the only effective form of social self-assertion. Even in civilized Europe at the beginning of the modern era the number of people crippled by violent acts was frighteningly high, while nowadays the incidence of violence is relatively slight, considering the availability and potency of various weapons. Of course the mass media would have us believe otherwise.

Once upon a time people would stream out of their houses, workshops and streets and hasten to the execution places, panting with eagerness to see living human beings drawn and quartered, put to the wheel, tortured to death. Today millions watch movies in which cowboys and gangsters coolly commit murder, but it would be sheer nonsense to equate the psychological impact of these scenes with that of public executions. In these films death is abstract; all that is realistic is the mechanical gesture which seems to bring it about. The observer feels much more like a witness to violence when he sees a simple brawl or a stabbing. Apparently it is the immediacy of the deed which makes an impression, not the quantitative degree of violence. There would probably be far fewer automobile accidents if drivers considered murder with an automobile to be an act of violence on a par with strangling or stabbing another human being.

Criminal aggression is at present much less widespread than in earlier times—despite the shocking mass murders occasionally perpetrated by individuals in countries where no limitations are placed on private citizens' access to firearms; despite the horrifyingly numerous cases of abuse, dangerous neglect and even murder of children; despite the relatively large number of crimes of passion. (One misinterprets the statistics if one does not take into account that the density of the population has greatly increased, that crimes are much more easily uncovered nowadays, and that news of them spreads to the most isolated villages.)

Those who see aggression as posing a greater threat to mankind than ever before are not thinking in terms of individual cases; rather, they believe that man as a species has become incredibly menacing and that any moment might bring apocalyptic destruction, since man now possesses an almost unlimited potential for utter destruction. We have had two world wars, methodically prepared by the most highly developed civilization in history; we have seen concentration and extermination camps established and millions of human beings reduced to a subhuman level, then gassed and cremated; several nations now have thermonuclear, biological and chemical weapons; and numerous dictatorships practice terror as a matter of policy while spreading the myth that violence is a liberating force. (This practice is especially characteristic of Third World nationalistic movements which employ the rhetoric of social revolution.) In the face of all these manifestations one cannot deny that the issue of aggression is crucial indeed. Nor do I intend to do so; I merely wish to raise a fundamental objection, one I once raised against Adler and other psychologists.

Every attempt to explain historical events psychologically is a grave mistake, like all forms of psychologism. One need only think of those studies that try to explain artistic creations in psychoanalytic terms or in terms of individual psychology. These studies should have been left unwritten, so little light do they cast on their subjects. The existence of class antagonisms, competition for raw materials and markets, wars as extensions of politics with other means —all these things can of course be examined from the psychological point of view, but that course might lead one astray unless one examines all these phenomena and events in their actual historical, social and economic contexts, using the appropriate methods.

Much of what happens when a war breaks out falls in

the province of the psychologist. What is the general mood
during the early days or weeks of the war? Why do people
experience a sense of triumph at the interruption of tedious
everyday life, a sense of relief? These questions deeply
concern the individual psychologist who has already studied
people's lives in peacetime. But war does not break out for
these psychological reasons, and it is not advertised as a
long vacation; instead it is justified by the governments involved as a necessary defense against the threat of annihila-
tion. And one should note here that Europeans reacted far
less enthusiastically to the start of World War II than to
the outbreak of World War I. The second time there was
no national hatred, no enthusiasm for murder and heroic
death on the field of horror—despite the usual propaganda.
In 1939 Europe entered the war in a resigned, even sorrow-
ful mood. One need only compare this with the photographs from 1914: never had one seen so many cheerful
candidates for death march off so joyfully into the void.

In actual fact the outbreak of wars is not psychologically
determined, except if they are wars between two small
tribes or clans; psychic factors do of course play a part,
sometimes quite an important one, but never the essential
one. During wartime social psychology has an opportunity
to study many phenomena that do not appear in peacetime.
But not one of these phenomena would suffice to explain
why the most insane of all great wars, World War I, broke
out and continued for four and one-half years until all the
participants were bled white. And likewise we must realize
that whether atomic bombs will be used or not by no
means depends on the aggressiveness of human beings in
general; or of the men who have to make the fatal decisions.

On the other hand, individual and social psychology

have a great deal to say about how a dictatorship comes to be established in a given country and manages to launch a reign of terror. What goes on inside the individuals of a nation when their people bring such a regime to power or allow it to seize power? How can one explain that in the course of only a few years a totalitarian dictatorship can reduce an entire population to such depraved complicity that it applauds all the crimes committed by the dictator and his clique in its name against "enemies of the people, subhumans and inferior peoples"?

What we have here is not aggression but the results of overwhelming, organized, permanent terror; people submit to it in order to protect themselves against its threats, then identify with it as a way of escaping a sense of humiliation and contempt for themselves.

And how should we interpret the fact that violence can exercise an irresistible attraction even as it frightens people off? Is man a sado-masochistic creature, too ready to use violence when it is not dangerous for him, and fascinated by violence when he himself becomes its victim?

From earliest childhood on everyone fears violence and learns to avoid it. But on the other hand, violence, whether perpetrated or suffered, is a source of intense feeling, and the absence of such feeling makes itself felt in routinized daily life, like the absence of salt and spices in our food; the lack need not be very distinct or painful, but it is there. Everything that injects intensity into our life seems to renew it. This fact corresponds to our ambivalent attitude toward everything new. I have already discussed neophobia, fear of the unknown; it has an equally compelling counterpart in neomania. The older we become, and the more automatically our lives unfold, the more we fear the new, but at the same time we expect something new every time we hear the postman's steps coming up the walk, every time the doorbell or the telephone rings, every time we open a newspaper or meet a new person. An orderly existence excludes surprises; it becomes fixed in rigid forms. All the more impressive therefore is the sudden outbreak of violence—all the more startling and all the more welcome. Why do millions read with bated breath detailed descriptions of acts of violence and fatal accidents? Because they want to "purge" their aggression, or "sublimate" it? That may seem a plausible explanation, and yet it seldom applies. In the past few years the readers of those very tales of accidents, fires and murders, especially the woman readers, have taken to spending considerable amounts of time and money on magazines and tabloids promising intimate accounts of the private lives of well-known or famous persons. Familiarity with details that mean little to the princesses, movie stars, singers and political figures themselves give a huge reading public an intensity which can be constantly revived without the necessity of deviating from the daily routine; the audience participates vicariously in the loves, fears, and pleasures of others.

Why do we feel this constant yearning for intensity, why we are always on the lookout for the new as if it could fulfill promises that no one has made us, as if it brought us satisfying answers to letters we have never written? Perhaps because even after we have organized our lives more or less satisfactorily we are still plagued by that problem that takes on different guises for everyone, that residual problem I have already discussed. We are incapable of *not* striving for perfection, incapable of establishing any lasting harmony. We always leave the door open a crack to let something unexpected in—the divine messenger bringing salvation, the missing element that will transform the tedium of everyday life. Even the most satisfying life cannot wholly fulfill us. We continue our search for that something, even resorting to prearranged misfortunes, the most varied forms of anxiety, happy or unhappy love, manias, hobbies, and a thousand other forms of activity or inactivity—trying to find that something extra without which everything else seems fragmentary.

A person may set up his life rationally and successfully; he may achieve a healthy balance between the active and passive forms of adaptation; he may largely overcome or master anxiety and reduce his aggressiveness to a safe minimum—and still he will have to accept the fact that his residual problem remains insoluble and unavoidable. He will return to the age-old question which has been expressed in many ways during the course of human history: the question as to the meaning of life. When a person cannot overcome an increasingly painful crisis and begins to think he will have to do away with himself, he comes to doubt that life has a meaning. In such a situation he finds comfort in debunking life; he proclaims that life is meaningless—simply because he despairs of giving it a meaning. Young people often fall prey to the seduction of this despair.

I have said that most human beings lose their ability and inclination to learn much too early, that they never really mature but wither on the vine. The residual problem is thus well founded, for in many cases what is left undone represents far more than what the person has experienced and accomplished. But in addition there remains the philosophical problem of the meaning of our lives, our deeds, our sufferings and our death. Adler and most of the great psychologists of our times failed to perceive the philosophical essence of this issue, or rather, they chose not to perceive it; perhaps they were right. But it is worth noting that a psychiatrist who was one of Adler's most talented students forty years ago, the Viennese Viktor E. Frankl, who went through the hell of the concentration camps, founded a form of therapy that is intended to help the patient find the meaning of life, or at least encourages him to look for it. He called it "logotherapy." But what if life has no meaning? Well, perhaps the search itself is enough to give one a reason for living. . . .

Part Four

Chapter IX

ABOUT SIXTY YEARS ago our century was dubbed the "century of the child" and the "century of the woman." Now that we have lived through two-thirds of it, we see it rather as the century of world wars, of totalitarian dictatorships, of atomic fission and of the most successful as well as the most unsuccessful national and social liberation movements. In addition it is the century in which every new accomplishment has been exhausted more rapidly than ever before; many more victories have quickly turned into defeats than would have been the case in times past, and in the end there have been no victors, only victims. One might also call it the century of psychology; its triumphs, too, may reveal themselves as defeats. . . .

It is not too early to draw up a preliminary balance sheet: What successes has psychology registered? Has it changed the nature of individual relationships? Can it be credited with transforming relations between the sexes and the generations? Has it influenced man's image of himself and his concepts of good and evil? Has it modified our ideal of personality? Did psychology spark the modern revolution in aesthetics, or was it only one of many contributing factors?

One might be tempted to answer the questions with a sweeping generalization: modern psychology induced or at least prepared greater upheavals than any other field or factor besides modern technology. Probably its impact surpassed that of any religion in history. Such a generalization appeals to our common sense.

It is an indisputable fact that seventy years ago psychoanalysis brought up the subject of sexual problems, that it ruthlessly revealed the gruesome side effects of suppressed sexuality, of repression, of inhibitions. And on the other hand we all know that by the year 1970 sexual freedom in the major industrial countries of the West has gone beyond the wildest dreams of 1900; freedom from inhibitions is taken for granted, and most of the old limitations, prejudices and prohibitions, often mistakenly called taboos, have lost their force.

From the outset Adler's individual psychology pointed out that authority was exercised in the family and the school as if its legitimacy were absolute and eternal, and that such authority had a deleterious, neuroticizing, extremely negative influence on people's capacity for life as social beings. Adler and all his disciples took up the theoretical and practical struggle against authority, mercilessly unmasking its harmful results, its stupid pretensions and its highly suspect sources. Nowadays authority has been so weakened that in most urban families, especially those of the middle class, it almost collapses once the children are old enough to resist it. Also, within bourgeois society the authority of the state, of institutions and their representatives, of dignitaries of every kind, of priests and teachers has diminished so greatly that it requires real audacity to demand recognition on the basis of one's position, prestige, diplomas and titles.

Freedom in the relations between the generations and the sexes, in the relationship to governmental authority and to the prevailing wordly and spiritual ideologies has been growing steadily; again, the resulting changes exceed those of any revolution. Lest I be misunderstood: in the phase immediately after its victory a revolution produces many astounding changes, but only during the first hours, days or months. Most of these changes do not survive, because the backlash that soon sets in suppresses the revolutionary forces—usually in the name of the revolution—to such an extent that finally only a few of the revolution's original achievements remain, and even these are often changed beyond recognition.

Did psychology produce this revolutionary century by changing human beings in a totally unexpected fashion? According to the "bang-bang" school, this is the case, as the story of the man who met up with a lion suggests. Shouting "bang-bang," the man held up his umbrella and took aim. The lion sank to the ground, mortally wounded. A miracle? At the moment the man with the umbrella uttered his cry, a hunter posted behind him fired his real gun. If there had been no man with an umbrella, the result would have been the same. But the bang-bangers, of whom there are many, stare in fascination at the miracle-working umbrella and have no eyes for the hunter and his rifle.

Increasing industrial productivity is continually modifying economic and social conditions in all sorts of ways. Among other things, they have robbed the family of its significance as a unit of production, except among farmers. The family has thereby lost much of its meaning as a social unit. The disappearance of the traditional relationship between the generations can be attributed largely to the two world wars, which prematurely liberated millions of young people from parental authority and drew women into industrial production, distribution and administration. The grave social and economic crises, the revolutions and counter-revolutions of the postwar era have dethroned age-old dynasties, especially in Europe, have profaned the old pieties, have destroyed belief in the divine right of the state and in the family order, hitherto assumed to be part of the natural order. People began to realize that nothing was sacred or permanent; everything depended on human decisions, and once human beings withdrew their support from a given institution it would collapse.

Was it perhaps the tremendous upheaval of World War I and the ensuing unsettled conditions that account for the huge popularity of psychology everywhere in the industrialized world? We see here what the Marxist would call an interaction of the material or economic superstructure with the ideological or psychic and institutional superstructure. The thesis of orthodox Marxism that it is not consciousness that creates social existence, but social existence that creates consciousness and thus of course also the unconscious makes excellent sense and is today less and less disputed. But the concept of social existence is already very complex. And the process by which this particular form of existence determines consciousness has hardly been investigated, even now, one hundred and twenty-five years after Marx first formulated his theory. Neither the Marxists nor those psychologists who concentrate on the relationship of social existence to consciousness have offered any new insights that might have helped explain the relation of sub-

structure to superstructure or the nature of their interaction.

From the Marxist point of view it is obvious that all
changes in the substructure determine changes in the relation of individuals, generations or the sexes to each other
and transformations in our social life style. Today modifications in our social existence are creating such changes
at an extraordinarily accelerated rate. One of the most striking features of the new situation is a change that has taken
place in the substructure, the displacement of certain socioeconomic factors with which nearly everyone was familiar
in childhood.

One of the least avoidable and most lasting impressions
used to be the experience of need. For all but the children
of the rich and powerful, the discovery that one simply
could not have all of the things one wanted constituted
the most common confrontation with reality. Reality to
most children was stern, stingy with gifts, an invincible
force. To give a rather banal example: at the beginning of
this century small children simply did not receive choco-
lates and other sweets very often; when they were given
treats, it was always in carefully rationed amounts or under
special conditions—the child had to have earned the reward. Thus a tiny crack opened up through which he
could peep into Paradise.

Scarcity has not been completely eliminated, of course,
and access to the consumer's Paradise is still controlled by
an individual's or a family's degree of prosperity; the door
stands wide open only for a few; it opens regularly for a
relatively small number, but for most it opens not at all,
or only on holidays and festive occasions. In today's affluent societies, the number of desirable objects or pleasures

denied the majority has been so greatly reduced during the past few decades that the experience of deprivation, once so familiar, has become rare and so has lost its fate-like implications. This helps explain why our present younger generation is the most indulged in history. In the past, each new generation saw the road from its desires to their fulfillment as unprecedentedly—and unfairly—long and arduous. Today most young people are spared this prolonged tension between their aspirations and actual conditions. A wish expressed is as good as fulfilled.

This new state of affairs is highly significant from the point of view of Freud's theories of human drives. It is even more significant for Adlerian psychology, which sees uninterrupted pampering and the resulting diminution of the need to compensate for and overcome difficulties must weaken the individual's psychic fortitude and social interest. Children whose every wish is fulfilled do in fact gain the mistaken impression that the position of the receiver is the only one appropriate for them; later on they will encounter considerable difficulties when they are called upon to act as givers in relationships that depend on mutuality. This is especially true of the sexual and erotic relationships of young people today. Now that women no longer need fear unwanted pregnancies, nature sets no limits to sexual indulgence. Young people are less and less inclined to accept arguments against any sort of sexual relationship, variation or perversion. This does not yet constitute total freedom, but license has been increased to a point unprecedented in human civilization except in times of apocalyptic catastrophe.

Does the practically unlimited lack of restraint on the younger generation represent psycho-hygienic progress? What role do inhibitions play in young people's lives today, especially in their sexual relationships? Individual psychology ascribes inhibitions not to repression and suppressed drives but to situations within which the child's schema of apperception develops simultaneously with his relationship to the world and to others. For an Adlerian, sexual and erotic inhibitions are merely manifestations of an individual system of reference, which in turn corresponds to the personal pattern to be found in every aspect of a person's conduct of his life. When sexual relations become as free and open as they are increasingly becoming these days, it is primarily a social phenomenon associated with the breakdown of parental and institutional authority. This breakdown itself results from something unknown in any previous civilization: the unconditional surrender of authority over their offspring by an entire generation of parents. The younger generation has won its freedom through abdication on the part of their parents, not by a militant act of self-liberation.

This parental surrender unleashed a movement which was to reverse the normal or rational order of things. Ever since our young people have become free, they have been in turmoil, rebelling in a manner intended to suggest that they must beat back a ruthlessly oppressive enemy in their struggle for liberty. With a flashy display of shadow-boxing they try to make up for a battle which, originally, they lacked the courage to wage and, later, had no need to wage. The need to think that they have won their freedom by their own efforts, leads youth to commit useless and pointless acts of extreme provocation. Modern youth keeps throwing off shackles which have already been removed. Freed slaves have often felt the urge to kill their former masters in order to transform themselves into free human beings.

Can one see the sexual freedom of the new generation as a sign of decisive progress in psychological terms? Would it be the equivalent of the psycho-hygiene derived from psychoanalysis? And to what extent do youth's hostility toward authority and their relative freedom from pressure by the older generation promote social interest and thus imply a marked improvement according to individual psychology's definition of mental hygiene?

Within modern student movements in particular a passion for social justice occasionally results in the formation of communities whose members make a very serious effort to replace their own individuality with a radical spirit of communalism. Is this what Alfred Adler had in mind when he called for community spirit and proclaimed that the fate of man hung on its being put into practice?

These questions are not easy to answer in the midst of a complex and ambiguous evolution. Any answers I give should thus be construed as statements of position, not as verifiable findings. A man in his sixties (as the author of this book is) should bear in mind that a wide age difference often makes it hard for him to understand those younger than he. Nor should he overlook the intolerance that sometimes springs up between age groups.

In ten or twenty years well-documented studies of the changes I have mentioned will become feasible; at about the same time those events will have been absorbed into literature, becoming mastered present and present past. In the meantime I should like to draw certain conclusions from the processes one can observe going on right now.

Modern discontent with civilization has nothing to do with insufficient access to various pleasures. On the contrary, it seems that the less such access is obstructed, the more inescapable becomes the insight that pleasure often does not provide happiness and often cannot prevent un-happiness. . . . This is of course no new insight, but as a personal experience it remained restricted for thousands of years to the privileged classes, and it usually became apparent to them only when they could no longer ignore the signs that the days of their rule were numbered.

But let us return to our previous question: Have seventy years of psychological influence made people psychically fitter for life, more perceptive, more capable of happiness? Do they run their lives more intelligently now? Do they see some meaning in life? These questions must likewise go without a definite answer, but one can safely assert that despite enormous changes in the substructure and the superstructure human beings are on the average no happier and no more unhappy today than in times past. They have rid themselves of many prejudices and have thereby become freer than their ancestors ever were. But what do they do with all their freedom? This question once troubled a numerically insignificant élite; now the entire younger generation is laboring under it, and it will become the central issue for all generations to follow.

Now that young people no longer have sexual inhibitions or taboos to contend with, yet find that unlimited gratification of their instincts makes them no happier, many of them face a boredom against which they have no defense. Many feel as if they were about to be sucked into a terrible void. To escape this feeling they resort to artificially whipped-up violence, to total social indifference masked as a concern for metaphysics, to indolent dandyism, or to the shabby nirvana open to those who substitute drugs for meditation.

No matter how one analyzes these phenomena, one fact seems clear: despite the astonishing proliferation of freedoms and the marked expansion of license, the sort of de-moralization that manifests itself as cowardice in the face of life has by no means diminished. It has merely acquired a whole new set of arguments to serve as pretexts. These arguments are directed against society, its order and its gruesome disorder—and many of them are certainly justi-fied. But in addition, today's young people exploit per-fectly good psychological arguments against authoritarian child-rearing and education, exploit them for their own purposes. One result of their protest has been the creation of a sort of illiterate parody of antiauthoritarian child-rear-ing, the permissiveness that became particularly popular in the United States. It now threatens to cause a pedagogic catastrophe of dimensions that can already be foreseen. Ac-cording to this theory, nothing a child does should be criti-cized, rejected or forbidden—supposedly because the child's personality must not be subjected to any outside pressure. The child must develop freely and completely. One could hardly imagine a more perverse caricature of psychological pedagogy in theory and practice than this total indulgence purveyed by nervous, insecure adults who seem determined to cripple their children's psyches from the outset.

This capitulation is not what we had in mind when years ago we young Adlerians demanded that educators learn to manage without giving orders and forbidding things. It was and remains true that one should not shelter children from life's difficulties, even from suffering. They must learn to master difficulties by their own exertions. In the realm of the psyche, everything worthwhile is a reward for overcoming obstacles. That is the point about com-pensation for presumed or actual, organic or other disabilities. That is the point about any form of training; first one learns how to learn, then one learns how to live.

"The best thing a fairy godmother can place in a baby's cradle is a batch of difficulties for him to overcome," Adler often said. The doorknob should be within the child's reach, not too high up, but high enough so that he must stand on tiptoes to reach it.

In summary, one can conclude that the teachings of modern psychology and the methods of counseling and treatment developed from them have had an excessively advertised but still healthy impact; its actual extent was determined indirectly and sometimes even directly by the major events of our century. The limitations of this impact have been pointed out, and I have tried to suggest the dangers that accompany the widespread misinterpretation and misuse of psychology we have witnessed in recent years. One should not exaggerate these dangers; but one should combat them as one of those new forms of obscurantism whose representatives claim to be and even believe they are preparing the way for enlightenment, unlimited progress and total freedom.

In times of stress individuals and peoples are often destroyed by that which is best in them. We live in such times. Part of the pattern is that the highest ideals are invoked while the very opposite is put into practice. One need only think of what happens when national and social liberation movements degenerate into totalitarian reigns of terror and sacrifice their ideals to corruption.

The only revolution in the superstructure that has lived up to its goals, the psycho-pedagogic revolution, has also been misunderstood and misused. But one should not forget that many valuable changes have been instituted, indicating that in the end no meaningful effort has gone to waste.

The unique community, known as the kibbutz, that was created about fifty years ago in Israel provides an example in more than one respect. Their young founders vowed to apply the principles of modern psychology to the education of their children. They wanted to produce the new man, who as an individual would be free of inhibitions and authority "hang-ups," and at the same time would see himself as an actively giving and receiving member of a voluntarily established community. Those young Jews, called *Chalutzim*, were mostly students, members of the *Hashomer Hazair* youth movement. They had come under the influence of psychology, psychoanalysis and individual psychology during the war years in Vienna. Enthusiastic promoters of the national renascence of the Jewish people, they decided to turn the bogs and fallow fields of Palestine into human terrain by the work of their own hands. They planned to found a new kind of human community in the spirit of Peter Kropotkin's anarcho-communistic teachings and the "Call to socialism" written by Gustave Landauer, murdered by counter-revolutionaries in Munich on May 1, 1919. They never betrayed the objectives of their youth; they founded their communal way of life. Only in the kibbutz, not in any dictatorship, have the essential features of socialism been made a reality: renunciation of private property, of money, of any sort of privilege. Everyone gives the community what he can, and the community gives each what he needs. This system would probably have disintegrated with the first generation born in the kibbutz if the founders' generation had ever relaxed its determination to pursue psychologically based pedagogy. But in the kibbutzim communal child-rearing and education have remained the foundation and the objective of this unique way of life. From birth to adulthood children have their own realm. The family has by no means been abolished; fathers and mothers become important reference persons to their children, but the community of children and youths remains the true milieu of each new generation. The kibbutz did more to realize the concept of social interest and community formulated by Alfred Adler than any institution before or since, and its existence does not seem to be threatened from within, although its future is tied up with the fate of Israel and the Jewish people.

The kibbutzim would be the best places to study the value of an educational system shaped by psychoanalysis, by individual psychology and by other modern branches of psychology. I need not add that although almost all authority has been abolished, there is no question of permissiveness in this system. I feel I can assert with confidence that the remarkable sociological and psychological phenomenon of the kibbutz offers proof that Adlerian pedagogic principles can be applied successfully outside of psychotherapeutic and remedial practice and outside of the family. It seems clear that it is thoroughly possible to maintain communities whose members are tied to one another by simple humanness, i.e., by a sense of community that cannot be destroyed by material factors or by personality conflicts.

Now I must try to at least suggest some answers to the last question I posed at the beginning of this chapter: Did psychology unleash the modern revolution in aesthetics? In times past many art theoreticians tried to explain the origins of Impressionist painting by reference to contemporary advances in physiology and one or the other of its new theorems. Similarly, other experts wanted to ascribe Expressionist art to World War I and the social unrest and political upheavals it brought. That was obviously a mistake, for Expressionism, like Futurism and Cubism, could be shown to have originated during *la belle époque*. When this fact was pointed out, still other experts came forward to declare that the various schools of art had offered prophetic revelations.

No one can deny that there is a very close, indeed unbreakable link between the various styles and functions of art, on the one hand, and society on the other. This question has been investigated as little as the connection between consciousness and social existence. Is it easy to measure the influence of psychology on the creative artist, who usually has no knowledge or only a superficial one of psychology? I do not think so. Conscious aims have a very limited importance in artistic creation. There are certainly similarities between what a writer intends to write and can picture in his mind and what he actually produces, but in most cases the two are not identical. What an artist thinks about art and what role he attributes to psychology is almost never of aesthetic import for an understanding of his work. Usually he puts together a theory which will justify all aspects of the work he has already created. On the other hand: long before psychology discovered the subconscious and its importance in artistic creation, unconscious motives played a role in art. Despite appearances, there is no reason to assume that their importance is any greater today than in the past.

I have already suggested that most attempts to interpret an artist's character and creations by means of psychology lead to a superficial and nonsensical analysis of the artist's neurosis, nothing more. But even those rare attempts that seem less ridiculous must be considered merely insignificant contributions to a better understanding of art. They provide further evidence that here, too, psychologism fails to focus on the object it claims to disclose.

Well then, has psychology remained without influence on the art of our times? Certainly not. But what has *not* had an influence on modern art—and what influences could it have escaped?

Has everything been said? Perhaps I have passed over the most important thing in silence. There are so many self-pitying individuals who, under the influence of therapeutic psychology, believe that they should use analysis and treatment as a refuge from all suffering, even meaningful suffering. If instead of dwelling on single cases of this sort, one sees all these (justifiedly) self-important people as contemporaries and considers what they have accomplished as such and what they have failed to accomplish, what suffering they have produced and what they have undergone, what is the end result of all these changes, and what should one think of this century of interpretive, educative and curative psychology? Has there ever been an epoch in which it was so easy to practice organized inhumanity? What about psychological progress, consciousness-raising, elimination of anxiety? Have there ever been so many millions of human beings who could be exploited for any purpose and degraded to silent, or even active and boastful accomplices in the most horrifying deeds? Has psychology prevented any of this? How about the other human sciences, and philosophy? I think of a world-famous psychologist who rushed to help the Nazis when they began weeding out his Jewish colleagues; he was ready to spring into the breach. I think of a great philosopher, perhaps the greatest of our times, who made himself the intellectual guarantor of the Nazis as soon as they came to power. I think of a Marxist professor of philosophy who proudly announced in the French parliament that he had taught his child to look up lovingly to the photograph of Stalin on his desk and say tenderly, "Little father." (I do not withhold these men's names to conceal their identity, which can easily enough be guessed. Rather, I want to mention them in this context not as individuals but as representatives of hundreds, even thousands, who acted as badly or worse. Where were such false witnesses *not* to be found? So of what benefit was expanded consciousness? What good has belief in social interest done?

In reality not one of the psychological schools has studied the central problem of the dual relationship of man to his deeds—his relationship as an individual and as a social being. Nor has anyone yet attempted to define the character of political man. No one, not even the psychologists, had foreseen how people would behave under totalitarian rule, and since Hitler's and Stalin's deaths the subject has not been studied much more thoroughly.

One conclusion seems obvious: like Marxism, which today's revolutionaries still invoke, interpretive psychology is really best suited to the people and conditions of the last decades of the nineteenth century. Today Marxism and interpretive psychology resemble young men with old faces, the avant-garde of yesterday or the day before. That they are not abandoned may be due to the fact that not much new has appeared in the meantime. Our era, the most talkative in history, keeps talking day in and day out—but it has yet to say what it is, or what it wishes to become.

Chapter X

I N JANUARY AND FEBRUARY of 1911 Alfred Adler delivered his three lectures before the Vienna Psychoanalytic Association in which he set forth the differences that separated him from Sigmund Freud. During the three discussion evenings that followed, the die-hard Freudians accused him of straying so far from their fold that he could no longer be accepted as a psychoanalyst. Thereupon Adler, who was at the time president of the Association, resigned from all the posts he held within it; with him several others quit the company of the orthodox, among them Carl Furtmüller; Alexander Neuer; Erwin Wexberg, the author of possibly the best introduction to Adler's individual psychology; E. Froeschel, later to become famous for his work in speech therapy; several other doctors; D. E. Oppenheim, who later chaired the public meetings of the individual psychologists; and Otto Kaus. They promptly constituted a group of "free psychoanalysts," as they called themselves. Some Freudians took part in their debates, but this angered Freud, who liked to see the line of demarcation kept as sharp as possible. Wilhelm Stekel, who had taken the position of mediator in the final dispute, joined the free psychoanalysts' meetings at first, as did Lou Andreas-Salomé, a personal friend of Freud's.

Of those who broke with psychoanalysis, none was as profoundly affected by the final separation from Freud as Adler. He experienced a deep sense of disappointment, and for a long time continued to feel the sting of many remarks made during the final arguments. But every meaningful rupture makes possible a new beginning, and in this case each day brought Adler a stronger sense of liberation. Adler continued to call himself a psychoanalyst, but in fact he had long since ceased to be one, and indeed had never been one heart and soul—in that regard Freud was quite right. In the months following the rupture, Adler wrote *The Neurotic Constitution*, and with that work came into his own. Adler was certain that what separated him from the psychoanalysts was more than a mere difference of opinion concerning the libido or the primacy of sexuality or the role of the will-to-power. It was a fundamental difference in the attitude toward psychology. Adler discovered that he was a radical individual psychologist who always proceeded from the premise that the individual was a consistent entity. Later he wrote about

that movement in psychology that I have called *"comparative individual psychology."* By starting with the assumption of the *unity of the individual,* an attempt is made to obtain a picture of this unified personality regarded as a variant of individual manifestations and forms of expression. The individual traits are then compared with one another, brought into a common plane, and finally fused together to form a composite portrait that is, in turn, individualized.[1]

Adler pointed out that the important psychologist William Stern—unfortunately too little recognized today—had arrived at a similar basic conception by a different route.

Adler was no longer interested in discovering the mechanisms that Freud considered so important; on the contrary, everything which could be regarded as a psychic mechanism was to be put into its context as part of the individual's total life style. Thus Adler did not examine traits, behavior and reactions in isolation, nor, and this was even more important, did he allow the sum of such manifestations to take the place of a comprehensive picture of the individual's character. It goes without saying that this holistic view is incompatible with the psychoanalytic approach. Only individual psychology provides a scientific, teachable understanding of human nature; psychoanalysis is neither inclined nor suited to offer such insight.

On the strength of his "Fundamentals of a Comparative Individual Psychology and Psychotherapy," published in 1912 as *The Neurotic Constitution*, Adler applied for a teaching position on the medical faculty of the University of Vienna. His failure in this attempt, a blow he never quite got over, nevertheless acted as a goad to compensatory effort. In 1914 Adler founded a journal of individual psychology, but after a few months its publication was interrupted by the war, for Adler was called up. During his service as an army doctor in Cracow, Brünn and finally Vienna, he found himself ever more at odds with the job imposed upon him: to certify soldiers who had recovered from wounds as fit for active duty; that naturally meant that they would be shipped back to the front. In agonizing dreams Adler reproached himself for the role he was playing.

Certainly it was these experiences, not only his socialist point of view, that caused his strongly positive reaction to the radical pacifism of the leftist opposition; right after the war he took a revolutionary stance in his brief essay, "The Other Side," and accepted the post of chairman in the Workers' Council that had just been formed. This period of rebellion did not last long—the councils disappeared from the political scene and Adler was soon fully taken up by his professional work. Around that time he gave up political activity for good. It is probable that the contact he had with Russian revolutionaries before and after the war had influenced his political views, or at least educated him politically. Raissa, the young Russian student Adler had married in 1897, maintained constant contact with fellow countrymen who like her had left their homeland to be able to study in freedom; she also knew political activists on the far left. Trotsky and Joffe were among the numerous Russian exiles and later leaders of the revolution who frequented the Adlers' house.

The very short period during which Adler became somewhat active politically had its consequences. Some years later when he wanted to enter Switzerland, he was refused permission; he had been blacklisted as a subversive. Adler never forgot this incident; the anxiety it created in him did not subside, as became clear during the years when he began vehemently to reject his Marxist collaborators and followers on the grounds that they would compromise individual psychology and interfere with its expansion.

During the ten years following World War I, Adler, by now in his fifties, reached the pinnacle of his career. More and more people flocked to him, impressed by his deep understanding of human nature and his genuine goodness. They were always repaid—Adler was always attentive and helpful in large matters and small, even getting up in the middle of a lecture or discussion to close a window because he had noticed that someone was disturbed by the noise outside or the draft. He was always a good friend to the very young man I was then; he was generous and at the same time made demands which constantly spurred me on. I should like to emphasize this point, for much of what I shall say in the following pages might make one forget it.

One can hardly imagine how active Adler was in those years. He had his psychotherapeutic practice, which was taking up more and more of his time and energy; for patients, far too many of them, streamed to him from all directions. Then he also worked in hospitals, taught at the *Pädagogium*, gave extension courses almost every evening as well as courses within his own circle, usually at his own house; he regularly took part in the weekly meeting of the Individual Psychology Association. (Attendance increased steadily, until finally only a large lecture hall could accommodate all the participants and audience.) He made lecture tours throughout Europe, and while on his travels took an active part in the spreading of the individual psychology movement. During this decade he wrote most of his books, of which *The Practice and Theory of Individual Psychology* (1920), a collection of "introductory lectures in psychotherapy for physicians, psychologists and educators" is probably the most important. *Practice and Theory*—one should note the intentional reversal of the usual order—is a book written by a man who never for a moment forgets that he is a doctor but who wants to reach far beyond professional circles. Here Adler had already found his new role in life, that of the educator to whom education is all-absorbing, the optimist who cherishes no illusions as to what man is and nevertheless holds high hopes for what man may become and, thanks to individual psychology, will become.

The first anthology Adler edited along with his friend Carl Furtmüller bore the title *Healing and Educating: Foundations of the Art of Education for Physicians and Educators* (1914, 1922). The authors of the thirty-odd essays were mostly former psychoanalysts who had gone over to Adler's side before or after the break with Freud. The volume also contained contributions by Aline Furtmüller, Ida Löwy, Margarete Minor and Hedwig Schulhof. In 1926 Erwin Wexberg edited the *Handbook of Individual Psychology,* in which one comes upon new names: Sophie Lazarsfeld, Fritz and Ruth Künkel, Artur Kronfeld, Ferdinand Birnbaum, Alfred Appelt, Karl Novotny, Otto and Gina Kaus, Alice Friedmann and Ada Beil.

This *Handbook* focused primarily on pedagogy. In fact, individual psychology chalked up its first really significant successes in this area—in child guidance, in therapeutic education and in psychological training for teachers. Thanks to the understanding and receptivity of the Viennese city administration and a series of organizations like the socialist "Friends of Children," and thanks also to the school reforms instituted by Glöckel, Vienna saw the gradual establishment of close to thirty public child-guidance centers, which not only helped children with learning disabilities and their parents but also many psychologists and doctors from the world over; through practical example these centers taught what theory alone could never have conveyed. In this connection one should mention the extraordinary and exemplary work of a woman who gave up her profession as a teacher to devote herself to this new field: Ida Löwy. Beyond a doubt she was the genius of the art and science into which individual psychological child guidance developed under her tutelage. Ida Löwy gave all her energies to this occupation. She possessed a remarkable skill for getting along with children and their parents, as well as an almost uncanny intuition. Anyone with the good fortune to see and hear her in action suddenly realized that psychological understanding and stimulating pedagogy are very closely related to musical sensitivity. By the music of her words Ida Löwy could inspire the confidences of both children and their parents. They could admit to their weaknesses, express—haltingly, and thus much more revealingly—their sufferings and failures. And the music which reverberated in the words of the children as a sort of undertone of self-betrayal told the listener more than the words themselves. Ida Löwy did not interrupt her work even in the face of a fatal illness. Her death at least saved her from the horrors of an extermination camp.

Among the chief pedagogic successes of Adler and his collaborators was a unique project carried out in a Viennese working-class district: an experimental school was set up in which the usual enterprise of teaching was combined from the outset with individual psychology's principles of psychohygiene. Oskar Spiel, the initiator and director of this experiment, and Ferdinand Birnbaum were the two most notable educators in Adler's circle; today their work is still generally recognized.

As I recall these distant times and places I keep wondering whether one would not do better to present Adler's views on education as the central issue, rather than his psychology and his theory of neurosis. His pedagogy shows very distinctly what unusual possibilities individual psychology could open up and how one might reshape family and communal methods of child-rearing to accord with the requirements of a social orientation and a new age.

Shortly after World War I Adler became convinced that the future of psychology lay in the United States. He therefore sought influential supporters in the large cities and at the major universities of America, in the hope that the headquarters of the individual psychology movement could be transferred there. He hoped to found physicians' and teachers' associations that would spread his teachings. Insufficiently prepared and with inadequate English, Adler set out for America to begin his one-man crusade. Despite such handicaps, even during his first trip he achieved significant successes. Lecture tours took him across the entire country; in addition he taught many courses and gave informal talks.

From 1927 on Adler taught at Columbia University and at the New York Medical Center. In 1932 he was named Visiting Professor for Medical Psychology at the Long Island College for Medicine. Three years later individual psychology had become well enough established for him to be able to found the *Journal of Individual Psychology* with the help of his American disciples. In 1927 his *Understanding Human Nature* was published in both German and English, followed two years later by *Individual Psychology in the School* and in 1933 by *Social Interest: a Challenge to Mankind* (English edition, 1938). In addition he wrote numerous articles and monographs for publications of all kinds, including his own journals.

Certainly much of what Adler published was merely a variation on his basic ideas, but some of his works show a gradual but real progress in the illumination of problems previously neglected or treated superficially. In the last years of his life Adler devoted many studies to the techniques of individual psychology, especially the technique of arriving at an individual's character or determining the objective and subjective factors pertinent to a given case. Adler often asked for short written reports on cases that were unknown to him; these he would read aloud to his audience. Sometimes he would interrupt himself in the middle of a sentence to explain what one should make of this or that seemingly insignificant detail. It was not unlike Charcot's method at the Salpêtrière. But this time the patient himself was not present for questioning; instead, a rather brief and unspecific report was analyzed. Adler wanted to demonstrate that such a report provided enough clues for an individual psychologist to pick out the essentials, the person's characteristic pattern, his unconscious goal, and—at least to a certain degree— the patient's formative experiences. Although *The Technique of Individual Psychology* offers a written record of these experimental guessing sessions, the reader who never attended one will have a difficult time forming an accurate picture of what went on. At first the procedure seemed irritating, like sleight-of-hand, but soon the attentive listener realized that he was witnessing an extraordinary application of the Socratic method. The most striking aspect of the performance was that Adler conducted such a revealing discourse on someone about whom he had only a few scraps of information provided by the doctor or someone who lived with the sick person.

Let me repeat here that nothing Adler committed to paper gives an adequate impression of his skill at establishing immediacy in a conversation or a lecture, at giving his listeners the impression that they were thinking along with him even when they remained silent. This skill was all the most amazing in view of the fact that, like all professionals, he used a relatively small, professional vocabulary. His command of language was much more impressive than he let on; in his writings one occasionally comes upon a passage that shows what he was capable of. An example is his essay on Dostoevsky in *The Practice and Theory of Individual Psychology*. But Adler generally paid little attention to the literary formulation of his ideas; perhaps he was always aware of how quickly time was passing and how much he still had to do.

Such thinking is surprising, for Adler had a strong feeling for form, in music as in all those modes of expression whereby human character both manifests and conceals itself. He advised his students: "If what the patient tells you sounds contradictory and confusing, close your ears and open your eyes wide. Watch him carefully as he speaks, and all of a sudden you will see what he is *not* telling you." Like great humorists and writers Adler registered almost imperceptible quirks of speech, gesture and movement; he was always receptive to any sort of comic effect and especially to what it revealed.

What I have said about Alfred Adler in these pages and many details that belong in that more thorough, less discreet portrayal that I shall never write, applies to the man I observed firsthand between 1921 and 1931. I knew him when he was in his fifties. Except during vacations and his travels, there was scarcely a day up until 1928 when I did not meet him at his courses, at meetings with his close circle, and at his regular table in the Café Siller, where his collaborators and most trusted followers gathered around him every evening. No matter how tiring the day had been, even when work kept him busy until late in the evening, he always came to the café and greeted everyone with a kind word. No one got up to leave until he had exclaimed, "Well, now it's no disgrace to go home."

Often I would stay on alone with him until well after midnight. We would go to one of the little eating places down near the Danube quai. Perhaps because his young companion knew how to listen and could convey hearty agreement or stimulating doubt with his eyes, the older man confided in him with an openness that he otherwise seldom had the occasion or the inclination to display. We had good discussions. Adler was interested in hearing what younger people thought about his ideas and about the various aspects of his movement. Another thing that I think attracted him to me was my ability to express these matters in a language very different from the professional jargon, and I did not deny that I often found the jargon very annoying. Later, after the rift between us, this propensity of mine disturbed him all the more, for he sensed in it a sign of treason.

What began to happen in Adler's circle had happened before in Freud's and in other schools, and it was probably not avoidable. In any case, its repercussions were most unfortunate. Adler's adherents, many of them former patients, were seized with the desire, usually unconscious, to form a sect. No sectarian can resist the temptation to clothe his admiration in the form of idolatry; in addition, his boundless devotion to the master takes the shape of marked hostility toward those who hold different views, especially those in his own ranks, whom he proceeds to accuse of heresy. This process had begun in Freud's circle by 1910 at the latest—and the sectarian character of psychoanalysis never disappeared, even after Freud's death.

Such a sect formed around Adler, and not only at his

table in the Café Siller. The pursuit of heretics and of
potential heretics began immediately. Certainly, some of
the more prominent of Adler's collaborators were likely
to defect, but this would have been avoidable. The more
their desire for independence manifested itself, the more
the sect channelled its suspicion that they wanted to betray
and desert Adler. And Adler mobilized his faithful with
almost imperceptible hints, which they always understood.
This was the sort of collusion Freud had practiced so successfully against Adler himself, against Jung and against
many others. And like Freud, Adler could not bear the
thought that anyone could abandon him. Like Freud, Adler
thought it was essential in such cases to anticipate the defection by expelling the defenders.

The "apostasies" attributable to personal motives were
not numerous and usually remained without repercussions.
More significant were those estrangements brought on by
fundamental differences of opinion. One such difference
grew out of the critical attitude taken by a few religiously
oriented colleagues of Adler's; these men were much more
put off by the philosophical weaknesses of all branches of
individual psychology than were the atheists or the religiously indifferent among Adler's following. The Catholic
Rudolf Allers and the Protestant Fritz Künkel, two in-
teresting and original thinkers, argued for religious points
of view that were thoroughly unwelcome to the others.
The final quarrel with Allers took place at a public session
of the Individual Psychology Association in Vienna; it
ended with his resignation.

Fritz Künkel had found much support among German
Protestant intellectuals; his books on characterology were
rightfully much admired. His *Introduction to the Study of
Character on the Basis of Individual Psychology* as well

as his *Vital Dialectics* are valuable contributions to both interpretive psychology in general and individual psychology's methods of character study in particular. Adler obviously knew what Fritz Künkel had done for him and his theories in Germany, but he always felt Künkel to be an alien in his circle and noted with satisfaction all the signs that seemed to point to the approaching defection. Thus Adler found the collaboration between Künkel and me all the more intolerable, a collaboration we kept up despite our political differences. Künkel, who had no personal ties to Adler, waited calmly for the rupture; he knew what direction he would take.

The other difference of opinion which disturbed Adler was political in nature, and political developments in Germany intensified it. Adler was alarmed at the danger to individual psychology which seemed to threaten from the direction of its Marxist wing. He accused his Marxist followers of hopelessly compromising his doctrine and systematically provoking the ire of the rightists and the Nazis. Adler determined to use all available means to destroy our position, or at least to weaken it so much that our entire influence would evaporate. Everyone had to know that we were no longer individual psychologists and thus had no right to invoke him or his teachings.

Adler underestimated the relatively important positions of the "pests," as he called us, and thus the difficulties associated with his undertaking. Otto and Alice Rühle, for example, had never needed to invoke the name of Adler, who meant less to their readers than they themselves. Rühle, a German by birth, was an old revolutionary socialist who as a member of parliament had voted against the war credits. For thousands of socialist educators he was the authoritative theoretician of proletarian pedagogy. Alice

Rühle, a woman of unusual intellectual prowess, had collaborated with Otto on several books, among them *The Path to We*, without doubt the best Marxist portrayal of the problematic aspects of individual psychology. In most of the cities of Germany and in several European countries we Marxists had been the ones to make individual psychology known. In the capital of Croatia, for instance, the doctor Beno Stein, the writer August Cesarec and many prominent physicians, philosophers and writers won over the young intellectuals to individual psychology.

Even before Hitler's seizure of power Adler had settled in the United States, but he visited Europe during the summers. The separation from Vienna and from his house in the Vienna woods must have proved painful for him. But he was so practical in his pursuit of a goal that he spent little time bemoaning his losses.

Adler's devoted friend Phyllis Bottome, in her biography of him, attempts to give the reader a sense of Adler's ceaseless activity. She does not fully succeed, and I would not even try. Adler always behaved as though it were up to him, and him alone, to spread his theories, which he saw as tidings that human beings needed more than their daily bread. He was surrounded by many faithful disciples and eager followers, but he wanted to bear the whole burden alone. Did he take it up because age was isolating him more and more, as it always does? I do not know; in those years we no longer knew each other.

A few of the ambitious had deserted him; quite a few believers and many Marxists had been banished by Adler himself. But there were other estrangements: some of the most talented left the sect or were expelled without ever becoming unfaithful to Adler's teachings. In Adler's eyes, however, they were lost.

Political events caused almost all of Adler's faithful adherents from Vienna and Germany to follow him and his family to America. Among them were Lydia Sicher, Rudolf Dreikurs, Sophie Lazarsfeld, E. and Helene Papanek, Alice Friedmann, and Leonard and Danica Deutsch. Adler's daughter Alexandra had early established herself as a psychiatrist. She achieved an important position, first at home, then at American universities and hospitals; her writings have always received the recognition they deserve. Kurt, Adler's only son, also turned to psychiatry; nowadays he devotes himself entirely to individual psychology and is one of its leading representatives.

Adler's eldest daughter, Valentine, and her husband were very active in the communist movement. After Hitler came to power they emigrated to the Soviet Union, where they became victims of a purge. Vali, as she was called in the family, was closest of all the children to her father, whom she resembled in appearance. With the support of friends, Adler and his wife Raissa made every conceivable effort to discover the fate of their daughter and if possible to secure her release. It was all in vain. Wherever Adler went, and he was always travelling, for one lecture tour followed hard upon the other, he kept hoping for the long-awaited letter or a telegram, for some word that would set his fears to rest. Not until after the war was it learned that Vali and her husband were no longer alive; she had died during the war, after years of imprisonment in jails and camps. When Adler was with others he managed to conceal his worries by means of feverish activity. Only his closest friends knew of the constant torment his daughter's disappearance caused him. His sole distraction was the movies, which he attended often: the darkened movie house allowed him to relax.

During a lecture tour to Scotland, Alfred Adler collapsed and died of a heart attack. It happened in the early morning of May 28, 1937, on a street in Aberdeen, not far from his hotel.

From earliest childhood Adler had had a particular familiarity with the thought of death, but unlike many philosophers he had refused to live with death in mind and to prepare himself for it. He certainly feared death, but he lived *against* it, so to speak. That remained his attitude from the moment he conceived the plan of becoming a doctor. And that is probably the reason that Adler, although a well-trained and diagnostically skilled physician who must have at least suspected the condition of his heart, had not guessed that death was so near. He had an extensive program laid out before him, one which would have taken years to complete. He still had much to do, as therapist, as teacher, as adviser, as lecturer, as director and organizer of the individual psychology movement, as editor of a journal and author of books he had promised to write, but had not yet done so.

In the last years of his life Adler had begun to ponder anew the meaning of life. He gave faith and metaphysics far more weight than he would have been able to ten years earlier. More and more his ideas circled around the creative powers of man—of every man, not just the artist.

Who can say where these partly new and unfamiliar thoughts would have led him? Who can say whether this sixty-seven-year-old man with his undiminished élan would have invited a new breakthrough—that breakthrough with which a human being gives his life an extra dimension that most people yearn for in vain, without which our fragmentary life often degenerates into a wretched piece of rubble.

Alfred Adler did not die in the America he had set out twelve years earlier to conquer; and he had not conquered it. The immigration of many psychoanalysts and individual psychologists, most of them Jews, transformed America into the Mecca of interpretive psychology, the center of psychotherapy. Sigmund Freud hated America, but there is no doubt that the country carried psychoanalysis to an almost total triumph; at the universities and in public opinion psychoanalysis gained ascendancy over all the other branches of psychotherapy, and the number of patients able to pay for psychoanalysis increased to an unforeseen extent.

Was Adler defeated in the competition he had sought? Many respected individual psychologists have gained success, and the teaching and treatment centers established by them in American cities have a substantial reputation. Pupils of Adler's are active and well known in Europe, men like Dr. Joshua Bierer, who introduced group therapy to England and made it popular. Despite these and many other successes, psychoanalysis has clearly won out. All the more so now that today's youth is becoming interested, although this interest is largely based on misunderstandings, like the young people's interest in Marxism.

On the other hand, Adler correctly foresaw that psychoanalysis would unofficially appropriate more and more of individual psychology's psychopathological conceptions, social perspective and technique of treatment and guidance. This process has been underway for some years now.

It looks as though this posthumous triumph might remain as unacknowledged as Adler himself always remained. That would be a great injustice, for Adler has insights to offer the world that are crucial to the formation of a true human community.

On June 22, 1937 Freud commented in a letter to Arnold
Zweig on the sudden death of his former collaborator:

For a Jewish boy out of a Viennese suburb death in Aberdeen
is an unheard-of career in itself and proof of how far he had
got on. The world really rewarded him richly for his service
in having contradicted psychoanalysis.[2]

This tells us more about Freud himself than about Adler
and his fate. We see not only the malice which old men
can sometimes hardly resist; we also see more of his character than all his psychoanalytic interpretation of symbols,
his foolish chains of associations and the whole game with
the libido and death and murder wishes and guilt feelings
could have revealed to us. For this reason, but not solely
for this reason, I shall refrain from using individual psychology to analyze his words on the death of a man fourteen years his junior.

According to his biographer Ernest Jones, Sigmund
Freud offers a unique example of a man who was able to
cure himself of his own neurosis, using only the theory he
himself had created. If one agrees with Ernest Jones, one
must ask what good such a cure is if it leaves the cured
patient capable of such glee at another man's death, capable
of such paranoid scorn. I have tried to answer this question, stated in more general form, in this book. Let me
record here a remarkable fact: in his eighty-first year, at
the height of his extraordinary world renown, Freud could
behave as though he had never heard a whisper of interpretive psychology, as though his self-exploration had not
even begun.

Is this true only of Freud? Does it not apply to others
as well, although to a smaller degree—to Adler, who could
not resist using the same methods as Freud when he set out

to combat the "pests"? And does it not apply equally or even more to so many psychologists, who think they are doing their best to promote human self-knowledge and enlightenment? What should one make of this distressing state of affairs?

Those who have sharpened our perceptions of the world and ourselves, Freud, Adler and many others, have still not managed to free us or themselves of the oppressive burden of the past. The new has not yet eliminated and replaced the old; it has merely been added on, often incorporated to already existing conditions.

Thus the miseries of psychology are the miseries of the psychologists themselves. Here we have the answer to the question I posed in my introduction. But what if this predicament were identical with the characteristic and seemingly inalterable predicament of mankind as a whole? Our history resembles the movement of a river which takes up everything in its path from the source to the mouth until it loses itself and its entire burden in the sea: the water of the tributaries, uprooted trees, corpses of men and animals, and so much else, disgusting and beautiful, old and new.

That is what our history is like, and what we ourselves are like. Adler saw, and saw through, man as a creature of incredible insignificance and incomparable grandeur.

Notes

FOREWORD

[1] The title of a long play about Austria during World War I, written between 1915 and 1919 by Karl Kraus (1874–1936). Kraus was a publicist and critic, chiefly known for the satiric journal *Die Fackel* ["The Torch"], which he wrote and edited unassisted.

[2] In my book *The Achilles Heel*, trans. Constantine Fitzgibbon (Garden City, N.Y.: Doubleday, 1960).

[3] *Alfred Adler: der Mensch und seine Lehre* ["Alfred Adler: the Man and his Teaching"] was the title of my first monograph; it appeared in the summer of 1926.

INTRODUCTION

[1] The Latin proverb says *"homo homini lupus."*

[2] The formulation stems from Friedrich Nietzsche and is to be found in *Thus Spoke Zarathustra*, Zarathustra's Prologue, section 3.

CHAPTER I

[1] Karl Marx, *Theses on Feuerbach* in: *Marx and Engels on Religion* (New York: Schocken, 1964), p. 71.

[2] Adler, *Studie über Minderwertigkeit von Organen* (Vienna: Urban and Schwarzenberg, 1907). [The English translation, *Study of Organ Inferiority and Its Psychical Compensation*, was unfortunately not available to me.—Translator]

[3] Adler, "Entwicklungsfehler des Kindes" ["Developmental Defects of the Child"] in: *Heilen und Bilden*, ed. Adler and Carl Furtmüller (Munich: Reinhardt, 1914).

231

[4] Sigmund Freud, *The Origins of Psycho-Analysis: Letters to Wilhelm Fliess, Drafts and Notes: 1887–1902*, trans. Eric Mosbacher and James Strachey (New York: Basic Books, 1954), p. 311.

[5] *Ibid.*, p. 298.

[6] Freud, *The Standard Edition of the Complete Psychological Works*, trans. under general editorship of James Strachey (London: Hogarth Press and the Institute of Psycho-Analysis, rev. ed. 1959), V. 483.

[7] Freud, *The Origins of Psycho-Analysis*, p. 219.

[8] Freud, *Standard Edition*, XX, 273.

[9] *Ibid., loc. cit.*

CHAPTER II

[1] Arthur Schnitzler(1862–1931) was a well-known Austrian dramatist and novelist whose works reflected the mood of Freud and Adler's Vienna.

CHAPTER III

[1] Karl Marx, *The Holy Family.*

[2] Adler, *Understanding Human Nature,* trans. Walter Béran Wolfe, 2d ed. (1927; reprinted New York: Greenberg, 1946), pp. 72–73.

[3] Hans Vaihinger (1855–1933), German philosopher, the author of *The Philosophy of 'As-If,'* trans. C. K. Ogden (New York: Harcourt, Brace, 1924), German edition 1911.

CHAPTER IV

[1] Carl Gustav Jung, *Modern Man in Search of a Soul,* trans. W. S. Dell and C. F. Baynes (New York: Harcourt, Brace, 1950), p. 79.

[2] Adler, *Understanding Human Nature,* pp. 72, 73, 74.

[3] Johann Wolfgang von Goethe, *Faust,* Part I, Prologue in Heaven.

[4] Nietzsche, *Human, All Too Human,* Part I, Aphorism 345.

[5] Adler, *Understanding Human Nature,* p. 72.

CHAPTER V

[1] Adler, *Understanding Human Nature,* pp. 153–154.

[2] *Ibid.*, p. 150.

INTERLUDE

[1] Nietzsche, *Beyond Good and Evil,* Part I, trans. Marianne Cowan (Chicago: Henry Regnery, 1955), p. 5.

CHAPTER VI

[1] Alfred Adler, *The Practice and Theory of Individual Psychology*, trans. P. Radin, 2d ed. (1925; reprinted Paterson, N.J.: Littlefield, Adams, 1959), pp. 23–24.

CHAPTER VII

[1] Hans J. Eysenck, "The Effects of Psychotherapy," *International Journal of Psychiatry*, I, No 1 (January 1965), 97–142.

[2] Paul Meehl, untitled article, *International Journal of Psychiatry*, I, No. 1 (January 1965), 156–157.

[3] Freud, *Standard Edition*, I, pp. 259–260.

[4] *Ibid.*, p. 260.

[5] See Chapter VI, note 1.

CHAPTER X

[1] Adler, *The Practice and Theory of Individual Psychology*, p. 2.

[2] Quoted by Ernest Jones in *The Life and Work of Sigmund Freud* (New York: Basic Books, 1957), III, 208.

Bibliography

THE PRINCIPAL WORKS OF ALFRED ADLER AVAILABLE IN ENGLISH

For a complete bibliography of Adler's works see Superiority and Social Interest, *edited by Heinz and Rowena Ansbacher. New York: Basic Books, 1956. I am indebted to this work for the details listed below.*   *—Translator*

1917   *The Neurotic Childhood: Outline of a Comparative Individualistic Psychology and Psychotherapy.* Trans. B. Glueck and J. E. Lind. New York: Moffat, Yard. *Study of Organ Inferiority and its Psychical Compensation: A Contribution to Clinical Medicine.* Trans. S. E. Jelliffe. New York: Nervous and Mental Diseases Publishing Company.

1925   *The Practice and Theory of Individual Psychology.* Trans. P. Radin. London: Routledge and Kegan Paul. (Also: Paterson, N.J.: Littlefield, Adams, 1959.)

1927   *Understanding Human Nature.* Trans. W. B. Wolfe. New York: Greenberg (reprinted 1946.) (Also: New York: Premier Books, Fawcett World Library, 1959.)

1929   *The Case of Miss R.: The Interpretation of a Life Story.* Trans. E. and F. Jenson. New York: Greenberg. *Problems of Neurosis: A Book of Case Histories.* Ed. P. Mairet. London: Routledge and Kegan Paul. *The Science of Living.* New York: Greenberg.

1930 *The Education of Children.* Trans. E. and F. Jensen.
New York: Greenberg.
The Pattern of Life. Ed. W. B. Wolfe. New York:
Cosmopolitan Book.
Guiding the Child on the Principles of Individual Psychology. Adler and associates. Trans. B. Ginzburg. New
York: Greenberg.

1931 *What Life Should Mean to You.* Ed. A. Porter. Boston:
Little, Brown. (Also: New York: Capricorn Books,
1958.)

1938 *Social Interest: A Challenge to Mankind.* Trans. J. Linton and R. Vaughn. London: Faber and Faber.

1956 *The Individual Psychology of Alfred Adler: A Systematic Presentation in Selections from His Writings.*
Ed. Heinz and Rowena Ansbacher. New York: Basic
Books.

1963 *The Problem Child: The Life Style of the Difficult
Child as Analyzed in Specific Cases.* Trans. from
French by G. Daniels. New York: Capricorn Books.

1964 *Superiority and Social Interest: A Collection of Later
Writings.* Ed. H. and R. Ansbacher. Evanston, Ill.:
Northwestern University Press.

The Journal of Individual Psychology, edited by Heinz and
Rowena Ansbacher and published in Burlington, Vermont, is the chief organ of the American Society of
Adlerian Psychology.

The Individual Psychology Newsletter, edited by Paul Rom,
is published in London for the International Association
of Individual Psychology.

Index

237